HAWKEYI

THE STORY OF AN ARMY PILOT.

BY

PAUL STRUGNELL

This edition published 2010 by One Fine Day Reading
www.onefinedayreading.co.uk

My story is dedicated to all those Army Pilots who have given their lives in the service of their Country and The Army Air Corps.

CONTENTS

To Steve

With Best Wishes

Paul Strugnell

Prologue.

The time was 11:15 on a cold, crisp January morning in 1983. The place, the county of South Armargh, Northern Ireland. I was on another of those interminable 'milk runs' over some of the most beautiful, yet foreboding country of that troubled province. Beside me sat a Sergeant in the Royal Engineers. In the cramped rear seats of the Gazelle helicopter sat another Sapper and a cook from the roulement Regiment based at Bessbrook. Our destination was Crossmaglen, or XMG as it was known by the members of the security forces. We were flying at 1500 feet across the icing sugar of the frost covered countryside. To our left stood the solid granite bastion of Sleive Gullion, rising majestically above the black and uninviting waters of Camlough, unruffled, silky smooth, perfectly reflecting the gaunt sentinel of the mountain rising in splendour above it. At 120 knots (about 136 miles an hour), we were covering the ground at the rate of two nautical miles a minute, and I knew from experience that, with the diversion of the approach into Crossmaglen, we had another seven minutes before we reached the relative safety of the stockade that surrounded the base. Every little movement, everything that struck as out of the ordinary, anything that appears to you as 'not as it was or ought to be,' demands that second look. You never get the chance to relax. The 'baddies' are ever resourceful and seem to come up with the most outrageous attempts to disturb the aurora of peace and calm that this country tries to lull the uninitiated into.

At last, the dull grey walls of the base loom on thc horizon. Not long now. A quick glance at the instruments for the umpteenth time today, not a conscious act, more reflex, but the eye and brain register all the information in a split second, all is normal.

Make sure the passengers have got all their bits and pieces with them. I don't want another unnecessary journey back to drop off something that they forgot to take with them when they exit the aircraft.

I sweep round to the north to make my approach into wind, and sight up on the 'H' of the helipad within the confines of the base, washing off the speed and height in one smooth movement. As we sink into the very heart of the base, the noise of the Gazelle hammers back at us from the protective outer walls of this distant outpost of sanity and order. We have arrived. Gently, I settle the skids onto the unyielding concrete pad.

"OK everyone, out you get and don't leave any straps dangling", I call over the intercom. The last thing in the world I need right now is to have a flailing strap-end thrashing around in the 120 knot slipstream and punching a hole right through the thin skin of the aircraft. The helipad handler, one of those special breed of men who devote such time and attention to ensuring that the right load, or the right group of passengers, depart on the correct aircraft, to the intended destination, comes up to the side window and hands me a bag of mail for my next stop off point, which I know from my briefing that morning is to be Forkhill, even deeper into bandit country and only about half a mile from the border with the Republic of Ireland. No room for navigational error in this part of the Kingdom. Another check of the instruments, a quick, but careful look round, to ensure that I am clear to take off, and I am `pulling pitch' to climb out of the protective cocoon of concrete and 'wriggly tin'. As the speed builds I turn east south-east, for Forkhill and the border. On past the incongruously classical form of the church at Glassdrumman and on to skirt the small outcrop of Croslieve, then it's a fairly steep approach to get in to the tiny, confined base at Forkhill. Once more, as I drop below the rim of the outer wall, the cacophony of sound reverberates back at me with seeming venom, but, to me the sound is a sweet one. Another successful trip. All I've got to do now is get back to Bessbrook, to a welcome cup of coffee and maybe a short break before it all starts over again. This is the unending round of trips that the Army has to fly in Northern Ireland in order to support the Security effort and to ensure the safety of our men in that Province.

All this happened only a few years ago, but we must go back to the early 70's, to when my story really begins.

Chapter 1.

A Dream Is Born.

My Story really starts amid the red brick, Victorian buildings of Norton Barracks, Worcester, in the early spring of 1970. At that time I was a Corporal Telegraph Operator serving with the 14th. (Special) Signal Regiment, Royal Corps of signals, having just finished a spell of seven years in Special Forces. For many years in fact, since before I left school, I had nurtured a deep desire to enter a career in flying. From the age of 16 I had, from time to time, done some gliding, encouraged by my elder brother John. The thrill of almost soundless flight was, to me, the most sublime of experiences. Even now I think that the ability to fly a glider is a wonderful way to learn the skills to fly a powered, fixed wing aircraft. It demands a special kind of anticipation and awareness that, quite frankly, is lacking in normal powered flight training. The last club that I belonged to was the Eagle Gliding Club at Detmold in West Germany. I think that seeing all those Army aircraft, both fixed wing and Rotary (helicopters), re-kindled my desire to eventually join, what I considered, that elite band of men that go to make up the Army Air Corps.

My first move was to approach my then OC, Captain Peter Hood, to assess the feasibility of my applying. As the resulting interview was favourable, I set about the mammoth task of wading through all the relevant sections of Queen's Regulations, to find out just what lay ahead. The initial hurdle was to overcome the fact that my eyesight assessment, as it appeared on my medical documents, was below the standard required for Army flying. Not to be daunted, I declared with great gusto, to all who would listen, that "I could see as well as the next man," and having shouted loud enough I was packed off to the Royal

Air Force Hospital at Cosford, to attend an appointment with a senior consultant optician who, after an exhaustive examination, declared me to be fit for flying duties. It was indeed a delighted Corporal Strugnell, waving his 'chitty' aloft that returned that night to Worcester. The next day or so were spent in a fever of activity filling in all the forms that went to make up my formal application to be trained as an Army Pilot. During all this time there was great rejoicing in the Strugnell household. It was wonderful to know that I had the full support of my wife Janet and my then 18 month old daughter, Claire.

Nothing happened for several more weeks, and then I got that fateful summons to see my OC, Captain Hood. He greeted me with an order to attend the Officer and Air crew Selection Centre at Biggin Hill in Kent. At last things were moving in the right direction. I had overcome the initial emotive barriers. I remember well the feeling of elation that morning when I set off by train for Kent. It was a fine day as justly fitted the occasion. The train journey from Worcester to Biggin Hill passed as if in a dream. When I arrived, those hallowed portals seemed to welcome me with open arms. I knew that I had made the right decision. The following two days of aptitude and medical tests seemed to rush past in a blur of concentration. Out of the 15 candidates on my intake, 7 of us passed. I remember the feeling of sadness I felt for those of us who did not make it. Of those of us who did, three were destined for the Army Air Corps Centre at Middle Wallop in Hampshire, where we were to spend almost a year of intensive study and wondrous joy of discovering our new found element. But more of that later. First it was back to Worcester and Janet, with the good news and a well earned celebration.

April 12th 1971 and we were off to Middle Wallop. All our possessions were packed and had been sent on ahead and we three drove down by car. Once more we had the task ahead of making a new home of an Army quarter. We had succeeded in the past and I had no doubts that, with Janet's help, we would succeed again.

Middle Wallop lies on the side of the River Test valley, about ten miles east north-east of Salisbury, between that most beautiful of cities and Andover. Who could have asked for a more lovely setting in which to embark on a new career? I remember that at the time I was suffering from a 'dry socket' and badly infected gum, having had a tooth extracted by a quack dentist in Worcester a few days before. In attempting a routine extraction, he had, in fact, not only broken the tooth and left most of the root in, but had also splintered the remaining tooth and then left these in the gum as well, with disastrous results. This was in fact to delay my starting the flying phase of training for about two weeks, much to my annoyance. It resulted in my having an unscheduled stopover in the Military Hospital at Tidworth to have all the debris removed. Not one of my most pleasurable memories. Imagine my frustration, lying in a hospital ward knowing that all my fellow students on my course were up there, not only airborne, but some of them actually preparing for their first solo.

At last my turn came. My basic instructor was a wonderful man, Norman Sharpe, an ex-RAF pilot with more hours and aircraft types in his log books than I could possibly hope to achieve. For 8 weeks he was to be both my mentor and friend. To say that he had the patience of Job would be a gross understatement. My actual flying started on 28th April, about two weeks behind the rest of my course as previously mentioned, and with his amazing patience and tuition, after several days of bad weather, with high winds and low cloud, that most memorable of days arrived when

I was to be trusted with several thousand pounds worth of Her Majesty's property in my hands alone.

No one can fully express in words what an embryonic pilot feels on his, or her, first solo flight. The utter fear, as Norman climbed out of the back seat as the aircraft sat on the edge of Andover airfield, the ominous sound of him doing up the straps behind me, then those comforting words of wisdom given in tones which relayed a calm certainly not being felt by yours truly. "Just remember to watch your speeds, and don't forget the swing on takeoff as the tail comes up". As he walked to the edge of the grass and on up to the tower to observe me I gently, ever so gently, started to taxi the Chipmunk to the end of the grass runway. Checks completed, I lined up for take off. Forward with the throttle lever to full power. As the speed built up I could feel the flying controls becoming effective, up came the tail and with relief, I see that, with the application of just enough boot on the rudder bar, the aircraft stays on course as the tail lifts. We are airborne. Now the shear panic starts. What goes up must come down. What if I cock up the landing, what if I can't land this thing at all, how long would my fuel last? All these idiotic thoughts flashed through my mind for a brief moment. Now it was down to the real work. Downwind checks carried out, I look down to see if I am in the right position to turn onto base leg of the circuit. Round I swing to line up on the runway centre line. Pre-landing checks, then as I sweep in over the fence at about 150 feet I see Norman standing by the side of the tower. I mustn't mess this bit up. Norman always insists on a neat three point landing and I not going to disappoint him. I gently round out and, to my great delight, I manage to pull off what, if you had your eyes half closed, might just pass muster as an attempt at a three pointer. No time for applause, it's throttle forward and round again for another two circuits. Having landed for the third time I started to taxi back to Norman, nonchalantly sliding back the canopy as I imagined that this was a World War Two Spitfire I was driving and not just a Chipmunk T10 trainer. I felt as if I had just conquered Everest single handed. Norman didn't seem too displeased either. As I said before, mere words can never describe that magical moment. It is something that always lives inside you. That was a truly memorable day that remains indelibly imprinted in my minds eye. It was now the real work began. Cross-country flights, aerobatics, low level flying and instrument flying were to follow in quick succession. It is at this stage that I think I should relate another memorable occasion, which was to serve as both a lesson and a standard by which to regulate my flying career for many years to come.

The course worked hard and played hard, and we used to troop off to a local hostelry once or twice a week for a bit of relaxation. Unfortunately, on this particular occasion, I over imbibed. The following morning, as I turned up for flying, bleary eyed and feeling much the worse for wear, Norman took one look at me and declared that we would do a session of aerobatics. Imagine my horror. This was the last thing I needed on top of my hangover. We went out to the aircraft, I did the pre-flight checks, all with this terrible feeling that 'His nibs' was determined to cure me of my foolhardiness. My fears were well justified. Several loops, barrel rolls, stall turns and spins later, I was feeling decidedly 'green'. The custom, on arriving back in dispersal, was for the student to run the engine down, which involved allowing the engine cylinder head temperature to fall sufficiently to switch the engine off. Well, I just managed to last out until the Gypsy Major died when, having first of all reached under the seat for the sick bag, I followed suit. I felt such a fool asking the ground crew where he thought I ought to put the now full paper bag. I won't bore the reader with his reply. I think you will have a pretty good idea, especially as he had, I'm sure, seen it all before. The pace had really hotted up now as there were more and more skills to learn. Our days were split evenly between flying and ground training. We had to learn all the necessary theory to back up our ever increasing flying skills. One of our ground instructors, who taught instrument theory, was affectionately known as 'Giro George'. His favourite piece of demonstrational equipment was a 28" bicycle wheel with a wooden handle attached to the hub. This he would use, very effectively, to show the properties of precession and rigidity possessed by a basic gyroscope. We must have been an evil bunch of bastards, as inevitably the thought dawned on us that this was fair game for a bit of fun. Some wag on our course, who shall ever remain nameless, decided to loosen the hub nut with the expected disastrous results. Sure enough 'Giro George' spun up the wheel by hand and, when he considered it to be running fast enough, he moved its axis and BINGO, the classroom was instantly attacked by a fast moving cycle wheel which seemed intent on destroying all in its path. We all rolled about in fits of mirth, unfortunately 'G.G.' didn't! I seem to recall that we all had a good wigging over this little bit of fun. Oh well, boys will be boys. The saddest thing of all was that one of the ground school instructors had a soft top MGB which was parked under the classroom window and the wheel, (which by now had exited through said orifice) crunched down on the hood of the pretty little sports car. That caused quite a few problems, which involved us digging deep into our pockets.

As can be imagined, the 'Esprit de Corps' among the members of the course was very strong indeed. We all worked hard together and, as previously mentioned, we all played just as hard together. The Army flying course is a mixed affair, with both SNCOs and Officers training side by side. As we were all going through the same problems and successes together, it was only natural that, to some extent, we felt as equals. This often caused problems, as often we would lapse into first name terms, much to the annoyance of the Staff. Having completed the Basic Fixed Wing stage of the course, we now learned of a bit of a bonus. As the Chipmunk T10 was also recognised as a civilian 'type', we had completed sufficient hours to qualify for our Private Pilots Licence. The Civil Aviation Authority also recognised the standard of our ground training, and having all applied, we duly received our little brown books that would have cost a civilian student a pretty penny. Unfortunately, mine has now long since lapsed. The next phase of the course was to prove one of the most difficult. This was our introduction to that magical beast, the Helicopter. I don't think I ever really knew the meaning of the word 'frustration' until this moment. Let me set the scene. A fixed wing aircraft, such as the Chipmunk, is inheritantly stable. That is to say that if you were to take your hands and feet off the controls in straight and level flight, providing that the aircraft is in trim, it will fly by itself and, to a certain degree, correct any deviations from its intended path. The helicopter, on the other hand is quite a different story. It is inheritantly ***Unstable.*** This means that given half the chance, when your attention is distracted by some outside influence, it will prove to you in no uncertain terms that IT, and not YOU, was really the boss. And all this just when we thought we could fly. The degree of co-ordination required to fly helicopters is remarkable in the extreme. I think it can be best described as akin to rubbing the top of your head in a clockwise motion with your right hand while at the same time, with your left hand, describing anticlockwise circles over your stomach. Not an easy task until the skill is acquired. Later in my career, when I was an instructor, teaching this degree of co-ordination in basic rotary instruction was to prove one of the hardest points to both put across and to be acquired by the student.

The particular helicopter that we were to be trained on during this phase, Basic Rotary, was the Bell 47G 4A. This was, in fact, the first commercial type of helicopter to be produced in any numbers. Designed in 1947, it is still to be seen flying in many parts of the world. One of it's greatest features has to be the incredible visibility from the enormous Plexiglas 'bubble' that protects the crew. It was probably for that reason that the Army flew the military version, the Bell 47G3B-1 (Army designation, Sioux AH Mk1), for so many years. But more of that later. Although very basic in it's design, the Bell 47G 4A, was a very good training machine as, like so many helicopters built since, it could be both docile.... and vicious. When in the latter mood it could, and frequently did, scare the pants off me and a lot of other people. One of it's vices was it's ability to show you just how under powered it was on a hot day in the middle of summer. Anyway, I digress. The main object of Basic Rotary Flight was to teach us the rudiments of helicopter flying, but in truth, in a civilian manner, using civilian instructors employed by Bristow Helicopters Limited. Their standard of pure flying instruction was, without doubt, second to none and I am sure that is the reason that they still do our basic helicopter training to this day.

The days wore on, and still I seemed to get no nearer to mastering the eccentricities of this obstinate machine. No matter how hard I tried to show it who was the boss, it invariably had the last word in proving me wrong until, suddenly, it all started to come together in some form of cohesion. That moment was to me as the divine light must have been to Saul of Tarsus, on the occasion of his conversion to Christianity. That night, I remember, was the first full nights sleep I had for many a night. From there on in, under the kind and patient care of my instructor, Ian McArthur, I seemed to come to grips with the task in hand. Now, I had actually come to enjoy this exhilarating form of flying. The helicopter is the ultimate flying machine, in that it can fly forwards, backwards and sideways with a degree of delicacy dictated only by the sloppy link between the cyclic and the collective levers…… the Pilot. There was much to learn and Ian, again, as with all the instructors who taught me then and later in my flying career, showed infinite patience. I have to admit that I was not a particularly bright student, in fact there were times when, quite frankly, I wondered if I would ever reach my 'wings parade'. One of the great characters of Basic Rotary was the flight commander, Mr. Sharples, who's two great claims to fame were his ability to teach us the secrets of the Bell stabiliser bar system (part of the rotor head), and his skill at reducing all those who flew with him to the consistency of jelly. He was a rather blunt spoken north countryman, but with the best 24 carat heart of gold I ever had the pleasure to meet. In a nutshell, his bark was far worse than his bite and many a student who was going through a bad spell has Mr. Sharples to thank when they reached their wings parade. I think it was his rather heavy accent that daunted most people...and the fact that he wore very heavy lensed glasses. He was a real gem.

Well, 80 hours of flying under the expert tuition of Bristow's instruction and I had at last learned how to fly a helicopter. I was a pilot but not, as yet, an Army pilot. That metamorphosis was to occur during the next phase of the course. Advanced Rotary, which now loomed large on the horizon. A further 8 weeks of intensive training, this time with military instructors, was to follow, but now to include the new tactical subjects of A.O.P. (spotting for the Royal Artillery guns) and tactical low level flying, what the Americans call 'Nap of the Earth'. This last item did more to excite and terrify me than anything that had gone before. It is the bread and butter of Army flying, and involves learning the techniques needed to approach a concealed hide area unseen and still be able to observe the enemy target without him being able to see you. Not an easy task. Coupled with all this you still have to get the necessary information back to base, either by radio or in written form. These were to be the skills that I was to rely so heavily on later, when I flew as a reconnaissance pilot over the next few years. At the end of this stage of the course was 'Wings Parade,' the award of the Army Flying Badge. This was the object of all the hard work. The ultimate goal that I had set myself which seemed so long ago, but was in fact only about 18 months before, when I was at Worcester. So much had happened since that initial interview with Captain Hood.

During this phase, and for the rest of the course, we were flying the military version of the Bell 47G 4A, the Sioux. One of the major differences between the two types was the fact that the Sioux was fitted with a turbo-charger. This gave the Sioux a greatly enhanced performance at high altitude but drastically reduced its power at low level. This fact led to a number of heart stopping moments when operating low level on hot summer days. One of the exercises that we were required to fly was to land the helicopter in what were known, euphemistically, as confined areas. These were generally small clearings, normally in woods, which appeared, to the uninitiated, to be no larger than your average sized postage stamp.

The technique for entering one of these confined areas was to approach to the lip of the clearing and then to steepen up the approach angle as you entered it. The big danger was to carry out the manoeuvre too fast. The net result of this mistake was that you required more power than if you used a slower approach speed. As I mentioned before, the Sioux was under powered in hot weather, and one of the most dangerous situations to be in with a helicopter is to be 'over pitched'. This is the situation where the pitch, or power setting, required to maintain a controllable rate of descent, demands more power than the engine is capable of producing. The result is a vicious circle. As the rotor R.P.M. decay, the natural instinct is to pull more pitch which requires more power and so on. In an under powered aircraft it is something you have to be constantly aware of.

Our military instructors were now filling our heads with the real purpose of our training, the tactical knowledge which was to be our bread and butter for the rest of our flying careers and beyond.

Wings day was getting nearer and nearer as each day wore on. Preparations were under way to get our wings, which we each had to purchase, and to prepare our uniforms with 'Velcro' press and touch, on which the Army Flying Badge would be attached on our wings parade. Boots and shoes were polished in true military style, and we each reported to the QM's stores to be fitted with our blue berets, the cherished head dress of the Corps. As with all specialist headwear, it must truly be earnt. Our big day was to be 21st January 1972. With great pride Mothers, Fathers, Wives, Sweethearts and Children, assembled in one of the hangers, to witness the ceremony of the Wings Parade. I don't remember all that much of it, except that I felt very proud to have come this far. Our 'wings' were presented by the Director of the Royal Corps Of Transport, Maj. Gen. Carter, and all I can really remember of the proceedings was marching out in front of the rest of the course, when my turn came and my name was called, to have my wings attached to the left breast of my tunic. I must have marched back feeling about ten feet tall. (I am in fact 5'6").

Afterwards, we all retired, with our guests, to our respective mess for a well earned celebration. We were now qualified as Army Pilots, but Middle Wallop does not give up it's babies that easily, and we still had to complete the last section of the course, the Operational Training Unit. This was the final polish, where we were able to practice our new found skills, in a Squadron environment, but still very much under supervision. It was an excellent system then which, alas, no longer happens. Now, sporting my new blue beret, and with my wings firmly attached, I was ready to go out and meet the world. But was the world ready for me? First of all there was a spell of embarkation leave to come as I was to be posted to 652 Squadron Army Air Corps, which was the Divisional Squadron of the 2nd Division, 1st British Corps, and was based at Bunde, in Westphalia, West Germany. I had thoroughly enjoyed my course albeit; I had from time to time wondered whether I would last the full duration of it. There was then, and still is now, a system, whereby a student may be RTU (returned to his parent unit) at any time during the course, if he fails to come up to the Army's stringent standards. I have, occasionally, seen grown men break down in tears when this option has been applied. Make no mistake about it, any man who gets through to be trained in flying duties is highly motivated to pass the course. It is not, and can never be, a slur on the individual who falls by the wayside merely because, for some reason or other, he finds himself unable to cope with a certain aspect of the training. The attrition rate is relatively low, but the high standards must be maintained in order to continue the Corp's fine record of flight safety.

And so it was, in early April of 1972, that I reported for duty in my first operational Squadron as the 'rookie' pilot. My total love for flying was born, as surely as the young toddler must, eventually, take his first stumbling steps.

Chapter 2.

The Early Days.

My arrival in 652 Sqn. was unfortunately marred by one of those interminable administration cock-ups that happen from time to time in even the best of regulated circles. Before leaving Wallop, we had all been instructed to write a letter of introduction to our prospective Commanding Officers. I had duly done so, about 3 weeks before my departure for Germany. It was just as well I did, for the barracks in Bunde are particularly hard to find for those who are unfamiliar with its location. About a week before I left England, I received a letter of welcome together with a detailed map of how to locate the barracks.

The confusion arose, it would appear, between the Squadron clerk and the O.C. Anyway when I reported on my first morning for the customary O.C.'s interview, I was greeted with the accusation that I had not bothered to write my letter of introduction. This I politely, but strenuously denied. After all, as I pointed out, if I had not written, how was it that I had received not only acknowledgement of my letter, but also the map showing me how to locate the barracks. I still had the map in my pocket at that interview. This did not seem to cut any ice with my new O.C. and if anything, only seemed to make the situation worse. I decided that the best thing to do was to just shut up and accept the (unjust) bollocking. Needless to say, I had quite a lot to say later to the Squadron clerk, who, it transpired, had lost my letter and then tried to cover up his mistake at my expense. The most unfortunate result of this incident was to be the souring of relations between my O.C. and me. He never liked me after that, but luckily I was only to spend a short period in 652 Squadron, before I was relocated at Munster, under the centralisation program, but more about that later.

Within a couple of days of my joining the Squadron, and after several flights with experienced members of my flight, I had to go through the ordeal of a Theatre Acceptance Check with Captain (The Honourable) Roland Hancock. [Now, Lt. Col. The Lord Castlemaine]. As the Regimental Qualified Helicopter Instructor, it was his duty to formally approve a new arrivals appointment to one of his Regiments' Squadrons. He was a perfectionist, and quite rightly so, and for about an hour and a half he put me through a rigorous check of all my individual flying skills. I passed, not maybe with flying colours, but at least I passed. The weather was fine and most of the days were sunny and warm. Just like the fledgling stretching its wings so I revelled in my new environment. I was now allowed to fly passengers.

Bunde sits on a plateau between the Beilefeld Ridge, to the north, and the Teauteberge Walde ridge to the south. There was an old and disused airstrip at Melle, about 6 or 7 miles to the west which we were able to use for pure flying training. The rest of the plateau was given up to farm land, not dissimilar to my native Suffolk, but with larger farm complexes. The buildings were very Germanic in their design with red brick mixed with a lot of exposed timber framing. It was altogether a very pleasing aspect. Bunde, the local town, was a higgledy piggledy mixture of old and new. Among the facades of the older buildings nestled newer ones of concrete and glass. I think of all my postings, both previous ones and those to come, Bunde was the least attractive.

The Army Air Corps location within the barracks was very small, so small in fact that we had to lift off from the dispersal area and then hover taxi in a high hover over a high perimeter fence, to a small field adjacent to the camp for take off. You will remember my reference earlier to the problems with the Sioux and its turbo charged engine with respect to hot weather and the resultant shortage of power. Well, this disjointed manoeuvre at Bunde caused a lot of problems and on a really hot day it could prove impossible to cross the fence. Later this situation was resolved by the introduction of a large section of the fence being given the ability to be lowered to form a 'gate,' thus doing away with the necessity of hovering outside ground effect. This certainly made life a lot easier for us Sioux jockeys. The Scout pilots never had the same problem as they always seemed to have plenty of power in hand. The Squadron consisted of 6 Sioux and 6 Scout aircraft at that time. I mentioned earlier about the centralisation program. Well, this was a move to centralise all the Scout helicopters in the Divisional Squadrons and the Siouxs moved over to the 2 Brigade Squadrons, then located at Osnabruck and Munster.

Those were idyllic days, spent in a mixture of flying training and 'taxi' work for the members of the Division, with trips to far and distant parts of the 1st. British Corps area. Our Colonel, at that time was one Lt. Colonel (Jimmy) Crow A.A.C. who in his earlier days had been in the Royal Corps of Signals. A strict disciplinarian, he was small of physical stature but a giant among those he commanded. He was immaculate in his dress and sported the most fearsome of handlebar moustaches. It was reputed that he possessed the divine skill to walk on water due to the fact that, when on exercise, he had the ability to appear, after walking across a dew laden meadow, without even a single drop of water on his highly polished boots. It was years before I discovered his secret which, it transpired, was entirely due to the special type of boot polish his orderly used. It all, however, helped to create much speculation among the troops, over the possibility of a previous divine existence.

It wasn't too long until I learned of the inherent dangers of flying in West Germany. Let me explain. In the United Kingdom, only a relatively small proportion of airspace is reserved for practising the art of low flying, which is equally applicable to fast jet aircraft and the slower, lower flying military helicopters. These low flying areas joined together by low level link routes are the only sections of UK airspace in which a military pilot may legitimately fly below 500 feet above ground level. In West Germany, although the same areas and limitations exist, there are infinitely more of them. One of these low level link routes just happened to pass right over the top of the helicopter landing site (HLS) at Bunde. It is never a pleasant experience, when climbing out of your home location at about 45 knots, to suddenly be confronted with the nose-on silhouette of a couple of Fiat G91 ground attack fighters at the same level as I was, but flying a damn sight faster and, having taken evasive action, to negate the certain chance of collision, I was even more horrified to see, quite clearly, the pilots of each aircraft with their heads down, flying on instruments and radar. Yes folks, adrenaline is indeed brown, I can promise you that. As this incident happened within a couple of weeks of my arrival in 652 Sqn. it was to serve as a cautionary warning for many a year to follow. West Germany is the exercise area for all the NATO aircraft (German, Dutch, Belgian, Danish, American, occasionally Norwegian, not to mention our own Royal Air Force), all vying for, it would appear, the same piece of sky. It can be truly terrifying at times. The first and most important piece of advice that I was given shortly after my arrival at Bunde was to grow another pair of eyes in the back of my head. I don't think my neck has ever been more supple than during my flying days.

April turned into May, and with great trepidation, having recently passed my arrival check, which event entitled me to at last fly live passengers, I neared the start of my first exercise in Germany. This for the raw rookie pilot is a terrifying experience. Will you be able to shape up to your new profession? How would you compare with the other pilots in your Squadron? All these questions would be resolved when you got out into the field to perform all the tasks that are required of you. All those weeks of Operational Training that you went through at Middle Wallop would now be put to the test, with a vengeance. Of course, none of your early passengers knew that you were so wet behind the ears. To them you were just another pilot. I well remember that first exercise. It was to take place, initially, to the west of Detmold, and then to work southwards towards Paderborn. The weather was to prove good and I found myself actually starting to enjoy this new found sphere of activity. Of course, I had been on exercise in Germany, with the Royal Corps of Signals, many times before, but exercising with the Army Air Corps is a much more civilised way of doing things. For a start, the aim of deploying a full Squadron of helicopters involves much ingenuity in satisfying the skills of camouflage. Just imagine the shear logistics of concealing 12 helicopters, plus a Squadron headquarters, not to mention all the other support vehicles such as the R.E.M.E. light aid detachment, cookhouse and fuel bowsers. It makes for a very interesting test of natural resources. Of course, the ideal locations are large woods or farm complexes. Needless to say the popular choice was invariably to go for the farms. It is a fact of life that anyone can be uncomfortable if they want to be. It is just as easy, however, with a little forethought, to be comfortable. Most of the farms in West Germany possess at least one large barn. These were to prove ideal in the housing of the H.Q. set up and also the messing and sleeping facilities. The L.A.D. and refuelling locations had, by necessity, to be located near to the area used to park the aircraft. The latter were usually, if no wood was available, dispersed under camouflage around the edge of a suitable field. If a suitable wood was adjacent to the location then the aircraft would normally be parked as near as possible to the edge of the tree line, at least 50 yards apart.

The job of selecting such a location invariably fell squarely on the shoulders of the latest arrival from the sausage factory, dear old Wallop. This could, and often did, prove very daunting to the rookie pilot. For a start, not many young pilots speak German, and even fewer German farmers in the heart of the country speak English. This led to not a small degree of confusion. If the task was not done properly, there was no surer way of incurring the wrath of not only the Squadron commander and his Squadron Sergeant Major but, if the accommodation wasn't up to scratch, the rest of the squadron personnel. As I said, it is a daunting task. Yes, you guessed it, as the rookie, yours truly landed this unenviable job on this, my first blooding in the German outback. What was in my favour, however, was the fact that, having spent already some 6 or 7 years in BAOR, I already had more than a smattering of the tongue. With this formidable weapon tucked firmly under my arm, I went out to meet the local farmers. The requirements were quite simple. A warm barn, fresh water, sufficient dispersal area for the aircraft and, most important of all, a porcelain toilet with flush. The latter was nearly at the top of peoples priority list. Thank goodness, for the sake of my colleagues, as well as for myself, I was nearly always relatively successful. Of course, while doing these recce tasks, one would meet the most interesting of people, as well as the most belligerent. On one occasion, after landing in the corner of a convenient field and walking the best part of a quarter of a mile, I was unceremoniously chased off the farmers land at the point of a shotgun. I didn't argue. I just left, trying to maintain as much of my dignity as was still possible under the circumstances. I later found out that the farmer in question had, only about a month earlier, had a full squadron of Chieftain tanks plough straight through a crop of barley on his land. I must admit, my sympathies were with him. I would not have been all that amused either, even though the said farmer would have been handsomely compensated, probably to the tune of more than the crop was in effect actually worth.

Exercises in Germany, providing the weather is good, can actually prove to be very enjoyable. The constant change of location and terrain, not to mention the villages themselves, made for a constant kaleidoscope of national flavour. Germany still has, to some extent, a feudal system of agriculture. Nowhere is this more evident than in the North German Plain. It was very easy to see the community as being of peasant stock. No one can deny, however, the general hospitality and kindness often shown to us. Bear in mind also that we were, in effect, invading their privacy and indeed, to some extent, their very homes. I sometimes wonder how the average British family would react under the same circumstances.

From the military side of things, the pace was always very fast. The morning would start with the inevitable dawn sortie, which would normally involve a recce to observe the area of operations for the coming day’s scenario. There is something very special about the feelings one experiences, having waited for the early morning veil of mist to clear sufficiently for takeoff, to suddenly, at 4 O'clock in the morning, burst forth into an unsuspecting world and to know that there would be no other aircraft in your area. The usual response was to switch over to the common air frequency on the radio and, in a gentle voice, utter the words, "Good morning world". Occasionally, if you were close enough to another squadron's location, you would receive a reply, often rude, from that squadron's early bird. To see the mist, still lying in the valley bottoms, or swathing broad fields in a cloak of shimmering white, while the trees, houses and churches reached for the clearer blue of the sky above, was a sight that never leaves the memory. Once seen, never forgotten. As previously mentioned, the bread and butter skills of an Army Pilot are the twin accomplishments of movement and concealment. This proved to be no mean task in the sort of terrain we often encountered. Much of the land was flat or at least relatively so, which meant that every small fold in the ground or stand of woodland had to be utilised to the full. I soon learnt that caution and not speed was the byword. It would often, for example, take the best part of an hour to cover the sort of distances that under normal circumstances would have taken only a matter of minutes. These 'first light' sorties were often undertaken with an observer in the right hand seat, whose task it was to look to the targets of the mission and to report back directly to either the squadron or to the unit we were supporting at the time. You soon learnt that to be successful, you had to work as a close team. This led to some very strong bonds between air crew. I have known grown men to enter into very heated arguments as to why 'their' observers had been allocated to another pilot.

Having completed the task in hand, another great pleasure was to return to one's base location for breakfast. Because of the early nature of the sortie just flown, you would often arrive back just as every one else was getting up. The benefit of this was that you were often first in the breakfast queue which had the advantage of your bacon, eggs, fried bread, sausages and beans all freshly cooked and piping hot, coming in man sized portions. Oh! how wonderful that repast would smell and taste, eaten as it was in the open air. After that there would be a chance, if you were lucky, to get a little bit of rest and relaxation before your name, once more, appeared at the top of the tasking list. The rest of the day would be taken up with a variety of tasks such as taxi runs, resupplies and of course more recces.

Every exercise would include a period of non tactical night flying. This was always an ideal opportunity to enjoy the countryside from a respectable height, often under a moon which enabled you to enjoy the scenery to a larger extent than would be possible when flying tactically. Even though I mention the pleasures of exercising in the BAOR area there were, of course, many little things that would rankle as well. The most distasteful of these, probably, was the constant smell of manure and silage while trying to enjoy a meal. Another was the damp cold of late autumn exercises, which brought stiffness to the body which at times could be almost unbearable. Under these conditions, it was always a blessed relief to get airborne and to turn on the cabin heating. Yes, we even had that most decadent of mod cons.

It was shortly after the end of this first exercise that I learnt of the imminence of the centralisation of aircraft which, I was to learn, meant that I was to be posted, yet again, to the Brigade Squadron at Munster. There were seven Sioux pilots in 652 squadron, and three of us were to go to Munster and the other four were destined to go to Osnabruck. The Scout pilots from these two locations were to be absorbed back at Bunde.

It was with a certain feeling of trepidation that I drove down to Munster in July of 1972. Although only about 40 miles from Bunde, it was like entering a new world. Munster lies in the centre of a large plain between the Teutaberger Walde ridge to the north, and the mighty industrial heartland of the Ruhr to the south, the smoke of which would often drift over us. Believe me when I say that the smell could, at times, be awful. Munster the city was as different to Bunde as the countryside was. It is an ancient city, steeped in history and full of architectural gems, not least of which is its 12th century cathedral. During the 2nd World War, the cathedral was almost destroyed by fire; not by the allies, but by the actions of the German forces themselves. Munster was a garrison town for the S.S., and towards the end of the war, when the writing was on the wall, so to speak, the S.S. garrison refused to surrender, with the result that the German troops themselves fought over the city. The net result of all this was to instil in the citizens of Munster a deep hatred for all military forces, including their own. Another of these buildings which is well worthy of mention is the 15th century Ratthaus, or Town Hall. The facade of which is richly covered with a multitude of figures and other decoration.

The Army Air Corps Squadron, 662, was co-located with one of the resident battalions of Foot Guards which went to form 4th Guards Brigade, the formation to which we were affiliated. They may have their own funny little ways these Guards chappies, but by heck there were many staunch friendships forged which, in my case at least, were to last right up to the present day. When I arrived in July, the resident Battalion in Waterloo Barracks were the 1st. Battalion Welsh Guards who, at the time, were away in Northern Ireland doing a 4 month tour there. Back in Munster, there were only a few members left in the Sergeants Mess where I was staying, until quarters were available for Janet and Claire to be able to join me.

To say that the Welsh members of the mess were extremely hospitable would be a gross understatement. Just to add a little more flavour to the situation, because of the low numbers of members 'living in,' it had been decided that we should use the Grenadier Guards mess in Buller Barracks next door, for meals. Again, the hospitality was superb. I seem to remember that during the weekends, the 'in thing' was to prop up the bar or, if that was impossible, to relax at a table consuming vast amounts of Gin and Tonic, interspersed with the occasional meal. These sessions would go on for the best part of the weekend. It really got to the stage that I was praying for a quarter to become vacant so that I could get back to a normal life style. Not that I complained too loudly!

I was soon to settle into the routine of a Brigade Squadron. There seemed to be a little more room for flair under the slightly more relaxed atmosphere. Maybe it was due to the fact that the squadron was the furthest from our own Regimental Headquarters at Lubbecke. This also had the advantage of equally distancing ourselves from Lt. Col. 'Jimmy' Crow. Much of the flying, other than training, was in taxiing staff from the Brigade HQ to go out and recce the areas for the next round of exercises. If it wasn't for the Brigade staff, then it would be for the HQ staff of the Guards Battalions or the Armoured Regiments which made up the Brigade. Life was pleasant, with plenty of opportunity to see a lot of Germany. The interim periods were spent in training. This would often involve taking an aircraft out to our local training area called Dorbaum, a large and sandy expanse of land on the outskirts of the city. In the summertime this could prove very interesting as it was also a popular place for the local courting couples. Surrounding the training area was rich farm land, normally under cereal crops. It never ceases to amaze me that, with love on the brain, couples could be so naive as to think that if they cannot see anything in a horizontal plane, then they in turn cannot be seen. This is, unfortunately, not the case, especially to a trained and keen recce pilot eager to prove that all those tens of thousands of pounds worth of schooling at Middle Wallop were not in vain. Picture the scene if you would. Young couple arrive in car. Young couple get out of car (usually with a blanket tucked under the arm) and, after a furtive glance round them (only taking in any information out to a radius of 100 yards or so), they slowly beat a path into the field of Barley or Oats.

With commendable enthusiasm, our young Army pilot is practising his skills of concealment. He is at a range of about 1,000 meters from the now parked car, and even more commendably, he has also spotted the young couple, with sufficient detail to even be able to describe their clothing at the subsequent board of enquiry. The secret was to wait at least 15 minutes before moving on to phase 2. This involved practising some hover maneuvers in close proximity, but out of sight of what we shall now term as the target (We have to keep a military sense of propriety). The target can hear a helicopter nearby but, not to worry, it can't see them so on with the play. Said helicopter now starts to combine some circuit flying, but away from the target. After about another 15 minutes of this lulling the target into a false of security, they have decided that nature must take its course. Now is the time for phase 3, the kill. Climbing to about 2,000 feet overhead, one can see the beaten path into the field. At the end of the path is the flattened area in the centre of which is the target, by now lost in the gay abandonment of love. By cutting the throttle and entering auto rotation, the Sioux makes very little noise. It is even less conspicuous to the fully occupied target. At about 250 feet, above the target, one would noisily open the throttle again and resume, in a nonchalant manner, normal straight and level flight. The effect on the target was dramatic to say the least. Items of clothing would be put on the wrong partner. The blanket would try to thwart their every stumbling move. In fact to put not too fine a point on it, what had only a few sweet minutes before been the closest thing they had to bliss, had in an alarmingly short period of time developed into a nightmare. A monumental cock-up, or not, as the case may be. It worked every time. Everyone a coconut, as the old fairground criers would shout

out. Believe me; they always left very much quicker than they had arrived. Oh well, it at least went to brighten up what could otherwise have been a very boring training sortie.

To get back to a slightly more sober level, October 1973 saw 662's first tour of duty in Northern Ireland. It was to last 4 months, but, in truth, seemed like a year. We were based inside the outer perimeter of Long Kesh prison and were mostly concerned with supporting the troops operating in South Armargh. It was, for me and for many others, an exciting, if at times frightening, environment. These were the halcyon days for the provisional IRA, who seemed to be having a lot of successes, far more than we would certainly have wished for. Life was a continual round of operational sorties involving a wide variety of tasks, ranging from recognisance to tactical night sorties using the Nitesun searchlight system. More of the Nitesun later.

One of the terrorists' favourite weapons was the culvert bomb. This could be as much as a thousand pounds of a mixture of home-made and commercial explosives, usually packed into a milk churn or empty beer keg, buried under a road, inside a drainage culvert, with a command wire leading to a safe area, well away from where the bang was intended to occur. They were very brave these forms of low life who masqueraded as freedom fighters. They didn't care who they killed or maimed. Military or civilian, it made no difference to them. It still doesn't come to that as witnessed by the appalling carnage at Enniskillen and other more recent sites. I have no truck with a small group of people (I refuse to refer to them as men), who do not even have the courage to face up to their opponents like men, but who instead hide in ditches with a battery and two wires in front of them and a short 50 yard dash to the safety of the Republic of Ireland behind them. They are, in short, Scum. Having witnessed the terrible injuries caused by these bombings, I speak with a certain amount of experience.

Our job was to patrol the roads at most risk and to inspect (from as safe a distance as was possible), every culvert or suitable spot as was practicable. It was never a popular task, but one that had to be done. We normally took a Royal Engineers observer who, hopefully, would have a better idea of what to look for than us. We later had various gadgets that would carry out this task far more effectively and in a much safer manner. The reader will I'm sure forgive me if I don't go into too much detail of these developments. My name is not Peter Wright.

Chapter 3.

In the land of Terrorists and Saints.

Northern Ireland is a province that has a certain magnetic attraction to all those who set foot in it. A land steeped in history and bigotry. A country where too much religion is practiced but sadly too little Christianity. Don't misunderstand me, there are some very good people in the troubled six counties. Probably more than there are bigots. Northern Irish hospitality is just as legendary as Highland hospitality. The bulk of the inhabitants are warm, generous souls, who are just as disgusted by the antics of the likes of the IRA and the INLA on the one hand and the UDA, UFF and UVF on the other. I draw no distinction between the factions of either side. A terrorist is a terrorist no matter what foot he leads with or what colour his or her cloth. To try to describe Northern Ireland, you have to have been well travelled in other parts of the United Kingdom. It is a land of striking contrasts. The lush green of the Clougher Valley and the water meadows of Lough Earn, clash dramatically with the harsh, barren moorland hills of the Glens of Antrim. Each in its' own way portrays some of the history of this magical land. A land where Potchine and The Little People still play a part in the every day lives of its' folk. The uninformed on this side of the Irish Sea tend to talk of 'Bandit Country', but it is my firm conviction that there is no such thing; just Bandits. Saint Patrick and Saint Colombo must be writhing in their graves at the atrocities committed now in the name of 'Faith'. Nowhere on this earth can there be a greater blasphemy. In a country so full of beauty, how can it be, that so few, can be so ugly.

The six counties, more commonly known as Ulster, are as different as chalk and cheese from one another. County Down, in the south-east, is a land of milk and honey, literally. It is the province's main producer of dairy products and arable farming. Mile after mile of rolling hills, interspersed with some truly beautiful small Loughs, undulating down to the sea under the towering shadows of the Mourne Mountains above Dundrum Bay. It is a magnificent coast line, with wide expanses of golden sand separated, in places, by secluded coves and rocky outcrops. It may be serene when the weather is calm, but in a southerly gale, the rollers and surf are truly awesome. It is a county of many moods. The winter brings with it a carpet of frost or snow which makes for some very spectacular effects in the early morning as the low wintry sun strikes a multitude of colours from the frozen loughs and flooded valleys. Then spring arrives, with the first blushes of new leaves and the lush grass where, but a short time before, there was nothing but the dull browns of the cold hillsides. Summer bursts forth with an enthusiasm unrivalled in this soft countryside. Oaks spread their mantles of green over the now ripening grassland. Cattle and sheep graze with no thought but to make the most of the bounteous supply of fodder placed on the land for their benefit. Autumn slowly creeps up and as if with a paint brush colours the trees with the artistry of a fine painter. On the sides of Slieve Croobe the stands of conifers declare their dark green foliage to the rest of the world, swathed as it is in the glories of reds, browns, and golds. Then once more winter, with her bag of icing sugar, carpets the land in white. County Down is indeed a poetical place but don't be fooled by its' serenity. The south of the county is as dangerous to the unwary as South Armargh. Tollemore Forest Park, on the outskirts of Newcastle, is the scene of several murders and sectarian killings. The Mourne Mountains are a well known training ground for the provisional IRA.

In sharp contrast, The Glens of Antrim in the north east are as rugged and majestic as the western highlands of Scotland, to which they were once probably joined. Mile upon mile of moor land tops separated by breathtaking glens sweeping down to the Irish Sea. Each of the Glens has its' own character, some, like Glenariff, have splendid waterfalls. Others, such as Glenarm are wide and roomy as if gouged out by some gigantic butter scoop. This awesome country continues northwards up in ever increasing grandeur up to the ultimate climax of the towering bastion of Benbane Head with its buttressed and gnarled face turned to resist the never-ending pounding of the Atlantic rollers.

Further round the headland after a short hop, one arrives at one of the wonders of the world, the Giants Causeway. The rock formations are truly amazing, stretching as they do out into the north Atlantic. In the winter this part of the British coastline must be one of the most ferocious places on earth. I have seen indescribably large rollers, relentlessly pounding the margins between land and sea.

As we travel even further westwards we enter the magical land of county Londonderry. Here, by contrast, the coastline is one of sweeping beaches of glorious golden sand. At its' western end, past Magiligan Point one starts to turn south-westwards and into the great bight of Lough Foyle, with its' rich fishing grounds and gleaming mud flats. On ever south-westwards, into the very port of Londonderry, once a thriving commercial centre now reduced to a trickle of small cargo vessels. Here the scene changes, to the west of the river the Bogside stand witness to the evil atrocities wrought by the IRA in the name of 'freedom', here walk the spirits of the murdered soldiers and civilians who died so needlessly at the hands of this vile organisation aided and abetted by their henchmen of the INLA. The sons of so many grieving mothers left to their tears in mainland Britain.

As we follow the river Foyle further south from Londonderry, we enter the county of Tyrone. A land of rich grazing pastures full of dairy cattle and sheep. On past Strabane and Omagh, skirting Dromore and Irvinestown and on into County Fermanagh with its' lakes and water meadows. This is the land of the River Erne with castles and stories of the 'Little People', of Potchine and coracles. To the west of Lower Lough Erne stands the escarpment, the only shelter for this gentle low lying lake land with the jewel of Enniskillen at its very heart.

Now, we must turn north-east, to clear the portion of county Monaghan, part of Eire, that juts like a great finger into the six counties, and follow the Clogher valley up to Ballygawly, again in Tyrone, before turning once more south-west and into County Armargh, both the most spectacular and the most dangerous 'bandit country' of the province. The names that follow will be familiar to any person who reads the national press. Down past Armagh city, with its twin cathedrals, on to Keady, Newtown Hamilton, Crossmaglen and then round to the east and past the lonely outpost of Forkill. Country that is perfect for the terrorist to operate in with its rugged garnet outcrops and soft valleys. In the centre of the area stands the 2000 foot mountain of Slieve Gullion, often shrouded in cloud or mist. Now we must turn northwards once more to pass the town of Newry, standing at the head of Carlingford Lough. To the east stand the Mourne Mountains, once more back into County Down. Leaving the mountains on our right, we complete our whistle stop tour of the province as we pass the highest point in the Mournes, Slieve Donard, below which nestles the holiday resort of Newcastle.

My description may have sounded at times idyllic, but don't be fooled, this is all potentially dangerous country for the uninitiated.

In the centre, or at least almost in the centre of Northern Ireland lies the largest inland lake in the British Isles, Lough Neagh. A vast expanse of fresh water, fed by five rivers and many more streams, but only drained by the river Bann. It is one of the few inland lakes that actually has its own fishing industry, with fleets at Antrim and Toome. Here they catch the famous Dolohan; a large species of sea trout much prized by those who are privileged enough to have tasted it.
Much of the operational flying in Northern Ireland is of a routine nature as previously mentioned but, occasionally, there is an incident which will spark everyone into a frenzy of activity. It is these incidents that make the time pass more rapidly. Most of the troops who go over there are committed to a 4 or 5 month tour of duty. There are, however, some people who are posted on a normal two year tour and who are permitted to be accompanied by their wives and families. These are the only people who can enjoy at least a little of the splendour of the countryside, and that only with the utmost caution.

This first tour for me was to be one of the 4 month jobbies, with Janet and Claire still safely back in Munster. It was a very long 4 months which unfortunately went over Christmas and the New Year. Suffice it to say that, apart from the spirit of comradeship which prevailed and the limited amount of booze consumed over the festive period, there wasn't a lot of revelry.

One of the more pleasant 'milk runs' was the Brigade SDS (Signals Despatch Service) runs which were made on a daily basis round all the main and not so main locations in the Brigade area. This consisted, in general terms, of visiting nearly all the unit locations in the counties of Antrim, Tyrone and Down. Bearing in mind my previous description of these counties, and the vast variation in terrain, and taking into consideration the perversity of the weather in the winter in the province, this sortie could prove to be a mammoth task in an aircraft only capable of 70 knots in the cruise. It was, however, the highlight of the day for the lucky (or luckless) pilot who drew the short straw. I enjoyed doing it primarily because it gave me the excuse to see the province in a reasonably leisurely fashion, from an acceptably safe height. The Scout jockeys, however, carried out the other ADS (Air Despatch Service, don't ask me the difference, it alludes me to this day), which was the same service but for HQ Northern Ireland.

Another task which I enjoyed immensely, but for a different reason, was the night flying exercises using the Nitesun searchlight to illuminate any scenes of 'nasties' during the hours of darkness. This was a most impressive piece of equipment, consisting of a 3 3/4 million candle power, steerable searchlight which could clearly illuminate an area the size of a football pitch from 1500 feet up. It was so powerful that, if you were to ignite it whilst still on the ground, it would melt the tarmac of a dispersal area. It obviously had to be used with extreme caution. Mentioning the Nitesun reminds me of an amusing incident that happened in the Mess one morning. We had several civilian women who waited on in the Mess, and one morning after I had been on a Nitesun standby duty at Bessbrook, in South Armargh, I was approached by one of these ladies, who enquired about the light she had seen in the sky to the south the previous evening. I replied that it was probably me, using the Nitesun that she had seen. One thing led to another, and being tired and in a rather impish mood, I mentioned that we had an attachment for the light that gave it the ability to see inside houses rather like X-rays. I knew that she lived in Banbridge which was en-route to Bessbrook, and by a process of elimination I managed to determine whereabouts in Banbridge her house was. After a few minutes chat, I happened to mention that she had been wearing a pretty night-dress the previous evening and as luck would have it

I even, purely by chance, struck lucky on the colour. She didn't speak to me for the best part of a month. I often wonder what she had been up to that evening.

Northern Ireland, at night, is totally different from any other part of the United Kingdom once the sun has set. In England, the way of life dictates that there are clusters of lit up areas, which obviously denote towns and villages. In between these centres of habitation lie great dark expanses of what is, in fact, often farmland. In Northern Ireland the picture is completely different. There are far fewer centres of civilisation and the areas in between, instead of having the appearance of a dark void, are a carpet of well spaced out individual lights which denote isolated farm complexes. The effect is very pretty, but it makes navigation at night much more difficult. One dark area looks very much like another, if you know what I mean. The one saving grace as far as I was concerned, was that if you got up high enough anywhere in the Province, you could pick out the high intensity lighting that surrounded the Maze Prison, within the outer boundaries of which was my Squadron's location. It stood out like a beacon in a sea of darkness.

Of course, one of the problems of night flying in Northern Ireland is the weather. Nowhere in the rest of the United Kingdom can the weather change more rapidly than in Ulster. The weather systems sweep in from the Atlantic and are met by the west coast of Ireland. The net result of this confrontation between air and land can be dramatic in the extreme. One moment can produce clear skies with bright starlight, and the next the cloud can creep inexorably in to obscure not only the sky but often the ground below. No matter how good is the science of Meteorology, there is always an element of guesswork. The trouble is that when you are observing some object on the ground, it is very difficult to maintain a satisfactory

eye on the weather conditions around you simultaneously. The results can prove disastrous. There must always come a time when the interests of safety must over-ride any tactical or operational considerations. This demarcation is a very fine one and unfortunately, once overstepped, the consequences are grave. More than one Pilot has lost his life simply by not abandoning a sortie early enough. I firmly believe that, "he who turns to run away, lives to fight another day". No-one will criticise you for using pure common sense. Not in the flying game anyway. Another killer is "get-home-itis". I'm sure we have all experienced that Friday afternoon feeling, where it always seems to be more acceptable to take more risks in the interest of getting home to enjoy the pleasures of the weekend. Well, in the aviation world the risks are just too great. Again, it has killed more than one pilot whom I knew. One of these incidents will be described in more detail later, in another chapter concerning my next tour of duty in Ulster.
It is amazing how slowly time can drag when the weather is bad and flying cannot take place. There were to be many such days on that first tour, probably because it was in the winter. I never knew such fogs as we experienced. They hung around for days on end sometimes. Thick blankets of swirling dampness that penetrated the body and the mind. For the R.E.M.E. fitters they were often a godsend, as they allowed much needed servicing work to be carried out without the normal pressures of having to be done 'yesterday'.

The services Nuffield Trust were very good in providing colour televisions and video recorders to nearly all the locations in the province, so these periods of inactivity were often filled by watching films on video, of which there were an ever plentiful supply. It took me years to be able see a film on television that I had not already seen in Northern Ireland. It was fine in the bad weather, but it could be very frustrating if you were on a standby duty somewhere, and right in the middle of a film you got a callout.

The Ops Room staff at Long Kesh were of a more sporting ilk, and decided that the one thing that we all needed was a crazy golf course on the piece of ground outside the Ops Room window. So, to a man, they set-to and produced one that would have done justice to any seaside resort promenade. It was truly magnificent. There were all sorts of obstacles to test ones skill and patience. And it was all free! There were one or two other distractions as well, like the goats. Slieve Gullion, in South Armargh, has a resident herd or two of wild mountain goats. Some-one, I forget exactly who, decided to capture one of these beasts with the aid of a Scout helicopter, and adopt it as a Squadron mascot. He managed to get hold of a magnificent Billy, who needless to say stank to high heaven, and even after the tenth attempt to scrub it down it didn't need a keen sense of smell to pinpoint it's location to the nearest square mile or two. This animal was to be christened Eric, and was the start of what was to become a considerable problem for the DOE, who were responsible for the running of the camp.

It was decided that Eric was a bit lonely for some goatess company, so without further ado a Scout was despatched to Slieve Gullion to procure a girlfriend for our lovesick smelly terror. It just goes to prove how ignorant we were about goats. When a Billy goat wishes to enhance his appeal to a lady friend, he has a rather repulsive way of going about it. He pees all over his stomach and chest! You don't have to be a genius to realise that this creates the most horrendous pong.

That wasn't the only problem, if you take one male goat and one female goat and leave nature to take it's course, you very soon have a lot of little goats all over the place. It was, for us, very satisfying to see the herd growing each time we came back on successive tours. At the last count in 1979 there were some 20 or more running around inside the camp at Long Kesh. It was at this stage that the authorities stepped in and decided that enough was enough. They were all rounded up and sent to good homes in the outside world. Or at least that was what we were told. One of the main problems of the goats concerned their insistence in sleeping under the portacabin accommodation occupied by the senior NCOs. It would seem that no sooner had you got to sleep, than there would be a hell of a commotion under the floor as the goats settled down for the night. Eric, in particular, having the largest set of horns, would make the most din. That, coupled with his aggression towards me when trying to make a dash for the shower block on a cold winters day, made me come to hate him. I wasn't one of those who mourned his passing. Another project that we, as a Squadron, took over was the care and feeding of about a dozen large brown trout which were kept in a static water tank (supposed to be used for a water supply for fire fighting), which was located just outside the main Squadron block. These trout had the most voracious appetites and keeping them fed with worms was a mammoth task. Indeed so time consuming was it, that one of our aircraft electronic technicians came up with a marvellous gadget nicknamed "The Wormer". This consisted of two metal prongs attached to an insulated handle and connected to the mains. When pushed into the ground and the current switched on, the effect was startling. All the worms within a radius of about a yard and a half, suddenly came out of the ground and stood on their tails. It was then a simple matter of going round and picking them all up and putting them into a Biscuit tin. It would take about twenty minutes to fill the tin which constituted a days feed for our dozen or so trout. It really was most effective. On subsequent tours of duty in Long Kesh, we were all saddened to find that the numbers of trout had diminished. On my last tour there in 1979,

I seem to recall that there were only three left. I suppose the temptation of a grilled trout outweighed the pleasure and challenge of keeping them. It always puzzled me, as a fairly keen fly fisherman, that the trout survived as well as they did, bearing in mind the still and relatively stagnant water in the tank.

It was very easy to get depressed and homesick on a four and a half month tour of duty in the Kesh, and that Christmas was the worst I think I have ever known. There were one or two bright spots, such as the tradition of giving the other ranks their Gunfire (tea laced with rum) on Christmas morning. This ritual was entered into with considerable gusto. Any hapless young squaddie who unwisely declined the offer soon finished up on the cold floor in a tangled mass of bedclothes. After all, if we had gone to the trouble of preparing the stuff, the least they could do was to drink it. The other highlight of that Christmas morning was to ring up the General Officer Commanding Northern Ireland, at his residence in Lisburn, and about eight of us gathered round the phone to sing "we wish you a merry Christmas". This was received in rather stony silence, and when we had finished, there was a polite enquiry as to whom he should thank for disturbing his mornings peace. Needless to say the request for identity was politely declined. He guessed anyway, because he sent us a New Years card with the cryptic comment to the effect that "thank God we didn't know any New Year songs." Christmas Dinner was served to the troops in the traditional manner with all the Senior NCOs and Officers waiting on us, and then we all, that is those who were not either flying or on standby, retired to the combined Officers and SNCOs mess for a well deserved drink or two, or three, or more. I took it fairly easy that day as Boxing Day was to see me on Nitesun standby down in South Armargh, at Bessbrook.

January passed with its usual round of various duties, and then at last February arrived. It was with not an inconsiderable amount of relief that the great day arrived when I was to go back to Munster in Germany and Janet and Claire. It was indeed a pleasant flight on the 14th of February 1974, when I flew my aircraft from Gutersloh, where the Hercules transport had landed us, to Munster, and home. I had successfully completed my first tour of duty in Northern Ireland and came home, perhaps mentally scarred, but physically unharmed. It was just the first of several visits to the province.

Chapter 4.

Growing Pains.

My arrival back at Munster was one of my most pleasant and cherished memories. The scars of a tour of duty in Northern Ireland take time to heal and it was Janet's care and love which kept me going through that most difficult of periods. It is hard to try to explain the mental torment that one goes through after a period of living on one's nerves for days and weeks on end and not knowing what lies round the corner of each and every sortie. The strain must and does take its toll. For four months I had been virtually as much a prisoner in Long Kesh as the inmates on the inside of the gaol. The same sights each morning. The same sounds of the guard dogs barking at the prisoners who baited them each night. The lack of darkness when trying to sleep, due to the thousands of arc lights which illuminated the Kesh when the sun went down. Now these and other restrictions were gone. I was able to walk down a street without fear. I was able to enter a bar just like any other person without the threat of attack. I could do all the mundane tasks, like shopping with my family and go to the cinema when I chose. All these things were a joy and a feast after the famine of four months deprivation. It was the same with the flying. It was as if someone had opened the gate and set me free again. It isn't that I didn't feel free in the air in Northern Ireland, it is just that the fear of the unknown was missing. Instead of having to worry about the terrorist bullets and missiles, once more all I had to worry about were the low flying military aircraft. By now my reflexes and 'sixth sense' were honed to razor sharpness. I instinctively knew when there was a low flying jet in the area, even when I hadn't been warned by some air traffic control or other. It is, as I said before, hard to explain the changes that a tour of duty in Ulster can bring about in the average man. In truth, I believe I had grown up as an aviator. By now I had something like one thousand hours in my log book and was in aviation standards coming to the end of my apprenticeship. There are a number of dangerous periods in a pilots career, the first occurs around the five hundred hour point, when the still novice pilot feels that there is nothing beyond his 'vast' capabilities, when in fact the truth is that his ambitions exceed his capabilities. The next dodgy period is around one thousand hours, my stage of the game, when pilots tend to get a bit blasé about flying. Piece of cake old chap. I am sure you know what I mean. After this, the next stumbling block is the fifteen hundred hour point. If a pilot can survive to this stage, then there is a very good chance that he will make a very useful pilot. There is a very wise saying in the aviation world which states that "there are old pilots and there are bold pilots, but there are very few old bold pilots." It holds very true, in fact I think I can count on the fingers of one hand the Old Bold Pilots that I knew in all the years that I was flying. Probably one of the greatest that it was my privilege to have known was Major Bob Bowles, a man in the very highest tradition of the ranks of army pilots. His great strength was the fact that he would only accept perfection. Whether it was in his own flying or that of someone he was checking out, the pass grade was only the best. He forgot more about flying than I ever learned. Of course, there have been others, and such is the Army Air Corps that there will be more in the future. Another more recent of the ranks of the bold, although I do not think he would thank me for the 'old' title, is Major Sam Drennan DFC, a man who is not only a great personal friend but also a truly fine pilot. It would be grossly unfair of me not to mention many more but, to be honest, it would take too many pages to list all those for whom I have the utmost respect and who undoubtedly will someday reach the hall of fame as regard the Old and Bold. To all those, I humbly offer my tribute. Incidentally, I would like to think that I was at least, in part, instrumental in inducting Sam Drennan into the Army Air Corps, when he was a Colour Sergeant in the 2nd Battalion The Scots Guards in Munster. I flew him on exercise once. I seem to recall that I had to return from an exercise location early one morning, pick up the Orderly Room Colour Sergeant (Sam Drennan) and fly him out to the exercise to join the battalion. The weather was typical for late September, with clear blue sky above and a little early morning mist below. Mist in the morning always thickens before it clears and, as we flew out to the area to the east of Detmold, Sam was intrigued to know how I could navigate with all that mist below us. Only the tops of trees and the higher ground stood out proud above the veil of white which still obscured the lower valley floors. I explained I was flying on a compass course which would eventually take me to a land mark (in this case a church spire), and from there on it would be relatively simple to find the Headquarters Company location. He seemed to be quite impressed, and asked more and more questions about the aircraft and the Corps. The bug bit him as surely as eggs were eggs. I hope he never forgives me.

As my experience grew so did my confidence. Now I was thinking less about the problems of pure flying, which were becoming more instinctive, and more about the military task in hand. This is the turning point for all pilots, whether military or civilian. It is, I suppose, the basis for the phrase 'seat of the pants flying.' There comes a stage when all pilots fly whatever aircraft they are current on, in a fluid and coherent manner. I suppose it can be related to driving a car. How many of us drive after a reasonable period of time with no thought as to when to change gear or when to brake with a degree of safety. All these things now become second nature. So it is in flying. It is at this stage of the learning curve when the true pleasure of the air is most apparent. The new freedom that it offers is like an elixir, a sweet formula of satisfaction. By now I knew with the utmost certainty that this was the life to which I was destined to enter. Nothing could ever replace the joy I felt every time I strapped into an aircraft with the knowledge that this sortie would be like no other that had gone before. It was around the eleven hundred hour point that I first tried to kill myself!

I was on exercise in the River Weser area in the east of the 1st British Corps sector, and had been tasked to recce the river itself, with a view to selecting a suitable spot for a crossing by a unit of Royal Engineers with a temporary bridge. As one can imagine with a brief like that most of my attention was firmly fixed on the river banks. That could have proven to be a fatal mistake. Just outside one of the numerous villages that are dotted all along the river was a steel cable strung right across the river at a height of about twenty feet. Just about the height I was flying the recce at. Behind the cable was a bridge, higher than the wire and almost entirely masking it from view. Luckily, I was only flying at about twenty to thirty knots and I did eventually see the cable at about the sixty feet range. As I pulled up to avoid it, I can distinctly remember a nasty smell in the cabin. Yes folks, yet again I had proved that adrenaline is indeed brown! Not surprisingly, whenever I flew anywhere near that village on subsequent exercises in the area, it was with a nasty feeling in the pit of my stomach at what might have, and so nearly did, happen. I never did report that incident for fear of what might have been (rightly) said about my poor standard of lookout. I suppose all this just goes to prove what a killer complacency can be. I certainly learnt about flying from that episode. Wires of all sorts and sizes, from thin telephone wires to high tension power cables have proved a nemesis for many an unsuspecting pilot, and not only rotary pilots either.

Life is one continuous round of episodes from which the wise can learn by their mistakes. This is never more true than in the world of flying. The thin dividing line between an accident and an incident is indeed slender. as my little episode on the Weser proves. In my case it was about five feet or so!

It was about this time, when I was maturing as a Squadron Recce pilot, that I experienced one of the most distasteful episodes in my entire Army career. I was yet again on exercise and during a lull between phases, it was decided that we should do a spot of tactical night flying. I was tasked to carry out a night cross country exercise with a relatively inexperienced Air Trooper ground handler as passenger. The Air Trooper in question was not the brightest, and as his personal weapon was a Self Loading Rifle (SLR), and the aircraft was fitted with dual controls, I had instructed him to leave his weapon in the Squadron Command Post for safe keeping. My order was overheard by a newly joined Pilot, a 2nd Lt. in the Royal Corps Of Signals, straight out of the egg, who immediately countermanded my order and told the young Air Trooper to take his weapon with him. One of the most important duties of a Pilot, no matter what his rank, is to exercise captaincy, and I considered it to be a flight safety hazard to carry this particular chap, in a duelled aircraft, at night, with an SLR. So I told him to carry out my first order and leave his weapon in the CP. This he did, and the sortie was flown without incident. On my return, having carried out the necessary paper work and gone to bed, I was woken up at about one in the morning by the 2nd Lt. to be told that I was to attend orders in the field that morning. At about eleven O'clock I was duly summoned to appear before my Squadron Commander. I was charged with usurping an order given by the 2nd Lt. and given very little chance to put my side of the case. I was in fact steam-rolled into being found guilty and sentenced to 28 days of duty pilot on my return to the Squadron base location at Munster. I was also informed that if I did not accept this punishment, I would be returned to the Royal Corps of Signals within the month. This was, I felt, a clear case of blackmail. Duty Pilot involved a considerable amount of extra work, normally in unsociable hours, in carrying out ground runs and air tests on the Squadrons aircraft after they had been worked on by the maintenance crew. I suffered the indignity of this clearly unjust sentence, and then did what I felt I had to do. I submitted a redress of grievance against my Squadron Commander, as was my right to do. This was unceremoniously thrown out and didn't even reach the ears of my Regimental Commanding Officer. What it did achieve however, was to completely bugger up the rest of my Army career. The Squadron Commander in question was, I later found out, a very senior Freemason. Sadly, The Army Air Corps is riddled with Freemasons and it is impossible to obtain the position of regimental Sergeant Major at the Army Air Corps Centre unless you are a Mason. The RSM always sits on the promotion board every year. It was all very ironic in the end, as he managed to kill himself and very seriously injure his crewman in Northern Ireland by flying into the highest point on a national grid power line, while trying to get home on a Friday evening from a period of duty at Bessbrook. A classic case of get-home-itis. He had displayed a total lack of the captaincy for which I had been pilloried. His death, unfortunate as it was, was not to be the end of the vendetta which continued within the Masonic members of the higher echelon of the Army Air Corps. I stayed a Sergeant for twelve years, even though highly qualified and in receipt of the General Officer Commanding Northern Ireland's commendation for my services between 1982 and 1984. There have been several very senior officers both in and outside the Corps who have come up against a brick wall when trying to discover just why I was not promoted, when they at least felt that I had merited it. There were many sergeants who were promoted from below me and who received a normal promotion path. Don't misunderstand my comments, I am not embittered, but I do feel that I was cheated out of what should have been mine by stint of hard work and application. I love the Corps that gave me the opportunity to fly, and that regard still remains. I suppose the greatest lesson that came out of the whole sordid episode, was that no matter how much in the right you may be as regards your actions in the Army, there is always someone who can screw up a promising career. It was shortly after this incident, that I very nearly managed to kill myself again.

Once more, on exercise, this time in the late autumn, I was tasked to go and pick up the Brigade Ops officer from a location in the field, where he had been attending a briefing. The weather was good but very windy, and I set off into the teeth of a strong south-westerly wind to fly to the pickup location, near Hamm. On arrival, and after a fairly lengthy search, I radioed back to my base to inform them that the passenger was not at the grid given. I was instructed to return to the Squadron location as it was shortly to move to a new position. Now, with a strong tail wind, I rocketed back to base. Halfway back I was given a new grid reference to collect my passenger and turned back into the strong wind yet again. When I got to the new grid, sure enough, there was the Captain duly waiting to be picked up and not a little annoyed that I had been so long in coming to fetch him. Off we set again, with the wind up our chuff, and as we flew back I heard on the radio that the Squadron move was under way. By now it had started to get dark and a fairly thick mist had started to rise. Not satisfied with messing me about below, the weather now had another nasty trick up it's sleeve. There was a fairly well defined temperature inversion which meant that the air around me was also getting a bit grotty. With only partial ground contact due to the mist, I managed to over-shoot the new location and, in the gathering dusk, found to my horror, that I was getting well and truly lost. I called for assistance from the CP (Comand Post) for a homing signal but I must have been out of range. The duration of the Sioux was about two and a quarter hours and I had been airborne for almost that time already. It was now completely dark, and in desperation I started to look for some lit up towns that I could head for, in an attempt to identify my position. There was one to my south-west, and I headed for it as fast as I could. I couldn't identify it from the map, so I decided that discretion being the better part of valour, I would select a clear area and land before my fuel ran out. There were two brightly lit areas, and going for the nearest, I was horrified to discover that it was a factory, criss-crossed with wires and power lines, and therefore totally unsuitable. The second proved to be a football pitch under floodlights, complete with twenty-two players, two linesmen and a referee. Setting myself up for an approach, I switched on the landing lamp and proceeded to shoot an approach to the centre spot. At about 200 feet, I saw the referee put his whistle to his lips and suddenly all the players started to leave the field. As my skids touched good old terra firma in the form of the centre circle, all the floodlights went out. I don't think I have ever been so lucky. Five minutes later and I would have been really snookered. As I ran down the engine, with the fuel gauge (which was notoriously inaccurate) reading a dcfinite EMPTY, the engine cut! Later when my nerves had calmed down a bit, I checked the carburettor drain valve and got about a tea cup full of avgas which was all that remained in the fuel system. I also learned about flying from that episode. And yes, the same applies about adrenaline. That, by the way, all happened on the 13th of September 1974. It was a Friday the thirteenth! I have always been cautious of Friday the thirteenth of any month since that night, even though I am not really superstitious. That night, I slept in the cabin of the aircraft, cold and pretty miserable, wondering what my OC and the rest of the squadron were going to say to me. As it turned out, I was only about eight miles from the squadron location, and everyone was very sympathetic towards me. In the morning, one of my colleagues flew out to me with some fuel and a filter, and, having put the fuel in the aircraft, we took off in formation to fly back to the rest of our little team and a well earned breakfast. It was worth some of the leg pulling just to be 'home.' The rest of the exercise went quietly and it was a blessed relief to get back to Munster and the family.

One of the things that one has to put up with in the flying game is the never-ending round of tests and checks that you have to complete to maintain your currency as a pilot. Six monthly flying checks always reduced me to the mental state of a plate of jelly. I have always suffered from 'testitis,' that not-so-rare complaint that reduces one's mind to putty and one's knees to rubber. I remember, at school, as soon as one of the teachers mentioned a test, my mind went a complete blank. How I ever managed to obtain the educational qualifications that I achieved is still a mystery to me today. Even routine annual medical checks produced a condition of blue funk in me. I never had a problem in giving a urine sample, the problem was how to cope with the over-production. Six monthly flying checks were ten thousand times as bad. It is each individual pilot's responsibility to ensure that all his checks and qualifications are up to date and, about a week before one was due for a six monthly, the onus was on you to ring up the regimental Qualified Helicopter Instructor, (QHI) and arrange for him to check you out. In fairness, these trips were as much for our benefit as for any other purpose. If there was some area in which one was a bit weak or unpractised, then it was an ideal opportunity to get any problems sorted out with an 'expert.' It took me years to fully grasp this principle and make the most of these trips. Our regimental QHI was, as I think I mention previously, Capt. Roland Hancock (now Lt. Col. The Lord Castlemaine and at the time of writing, Chief Flying Instructor at Middle Wallop), and it would be either a case of flying up to our Regimental HQ at Lubbecke to pick him up or, if there were more than one check for him to carry out, he would come down to us for a day or so. You simply cannot imagine the utter panic that would ensue when the fateful message came over the phone from our tower that the QHI was inbound and expected to be with us in five minutes. It was like the knell of doom. Once on the ground this mystical figure, something akin to the divine being, would take you to one side in the flight planning room and discuss what would be the profile of the check ride you were about to undertake. It would normally consist of a short cross country flight followed by some tactical exercise and end up with a session of emergencies and engine off landings on the Dorbaum training area. The whole thing would last between an hour and a quarter and an hour and a half. If it went any longer, then you knew you were in for a pretty uncomfortable de-briefing. As much as being a chance to practice things that were normally not allowed when solo, such as engine off landings, it was also a good opportunity for the QHI to iron out any bad habits which might have developed since your last check ride. I think that it was only when I became a QHI myself in later years that I fully appreciated the value of these trips. Most QHIs would throw in a few surprises, not to be nasty, but simply to make sure that you were prepared for anything. One thing that always amazed me was the incredibly smooth and accurate way in which any of the QHI's demonstrations were flown. I later learnt that, for a QHI, perfection was the only acceptable standard as far as his own flying was concerned, and the hope was that this would brush off on to his student. At the end of the gruelling experience, and having landed back at base, the next hour or so would be taken up with an exhaustive de-briefing, during which all the exercises flown would be examined and, where necessary, corrected. The end result, hopefully, would be that you were less likely to kill yourself for at least another six months.

On top of these routine six monthly checks, every year or so the Standards Team, (the QHIs responsible for the overall standard of flying throughout the Army Air Corps and trained to a Tri-Service level), would descend upon a proportion of pilots, picked at random, to assess the overall standard. If a regimental QHI could reduce me to a state of jelly, just imagine what these 'supergods' could do to my constitution! I was fortunate it only happened to me a couple of times during my normal squadron service. Of course later, when I was also a QHI, it was the standards team who gave me my periodical checks. Strangely enough, I always enjoyed my check rides as a QHI. I think that being able to see both sides of the coin makes a big difference to one's approach to these occasions.

In January 1975 I was offered the opportunity to attend one of the Royal Air Force winter survival courses at Bad Kohl Grub, in Bavaria. This was, for me, a wonderful chance to learn a little about the art of survival in sub zero conditions. I had already, in my previous service with Royal Signals and Special Forces, learnt some of the techniques required to survive in desert and jungle conditions and this would, as far as I was concerned, complete the trio.

Off I went by coach to this charming little Bavarian village set among the southern hills not far from Ober Amergau (famous for its passion plays). The weather was suitably wintry, with lots of snow and night temperatures dropping to minus 18 degrees centigrade.

The first part of the course, which was to last for ten days, was a mixture of classroom tuition and skiing. I was no stranger to the skiing side of things, and the tuition was mostly common sense. The biggest killer in a survival situation is ignorance. Armed with the correct knowledge, no one is unable to survive and survive in a reasonable state of comfort. There is an old saying that anyone can be uncomfortable but with just a little more effort they could just as easily live like a King.

The membership of the course was made up of 27 RAF air crew and yours truly. The RAF members were a mixture of fighter, transport and helicopter crews and, quite naturally, I was teamed up with two other helicopter (Wessex) pilots. We were looked after and taught by the best experts in the world when it comes to the art of survival, the instructors from RAF Mountbatten at Plymouth. Their leading light, on the instructional side, was a very wise Geordie flight sergeant with a sense of humour that would have done credit in the silent movies. Dry wasn't the word for it. His sense of humour was positively arid. We learnt about equipment, movement, trapping and preparing food and escape and evasion, all spread over the first six days. Each afternoon during this period would be spent on the surrounding slopes with our two German ski instructors. You could describe this period as the honeymoon; the really hard time was yet to come. On the seventh day, we were all issued with a parachute and dinghy pack and told to get on with preparing the same for a survival exercise in the adjoining hills. The parachutes were hastily modified into sleeping bags, with enough material left over to furnish a shelter of sorts, and the dinghy was either discarded in favour of its pack, or kept for use as insulation against the cold. Of course the penalty for the added comfort of keeping it was, certainly in my case, offset by the penalty of additional weight to be carried. I opted to simply retain the pack. We were then issued with a tin of glucose sweets, as issued in the dinghy pack and, dressed in our two piece Mk 3 winter flying suits, and having been first searched to ensure we didn't have such things as soup powder or chocolate bars secreted about our persons, we were herded onto a bus for our short trip out to the exercise area. At set intervals along the road, we were dumped off to make our way, in pairs to the assembly area, where we were to spend the first night. On arrival, our first priority was to gather as much in the way of dry wood as was possible before nightfall in order to get a fire going. This achieved, and with the aid of an old tin can found in the search for kindling, I proceeded to boil some water together with a couple of the precious glucose sweets, to make an acceptably warming drink. This inside me, I then set to and produced a shelter of sorts into which I crawled with my parachute sleeping bag. I might add that the parachutes were all old and condemned ones, and for some lucky people, of which I was one, these proved to be silk jobs and not the modern nylon ones. These, believe me, are much warmer than their modern counterparts. I spent a comfortable night, and in the morning, sucking once more on a glucose sweet, we set off further into the woods to our next exercise area. This time we were matched up by aircraft type to simulate a crew situation, and left to the serious business of survival in groups of twos and threes. The first priority was to carry out a recce of the area to see if any of the previous courses had obliged us by leaving anything behind. No such luck. The directing staff had obviously swept the ground pretty thoroughly. I forgot to mention that, before we were set loose on the scene, we were allowed to make up a small survival tin to be carried in the leg pocket of our flying suits. Mine consisted, rather optimistically, of a few snares, some light twine, and some fishing line and a couple of hooks. Just down the hill from our allocated location was a rather small drainage canal cut into the hillside and properly brick banked. Ah ha! thinks I, where there is water there just possibly could be fish, and already I was hungry. Down I went with my fishing line and hooks to set up a couple of night lines. Just as I had finished setting them, along came our Geordie flight sergeant instructor, with the dry comment that HE had been coming here for donkeys years and to the best of his knowledge, no-one had ever caught so much as a cold out of that canal. Remember what I said about ignorance being your greatest enemy in a survival situation? Well I was hungry and that can impel one to carry on in the certain knowledge that 'nothing ventured, nothing gained.' Off Geordie went, muttering something about stupid Pongos and pipe dreams and I finished off setting my lines.

Back to the camp area and the interminable search for firewood. We were not allowed to cut down any timber and so we had to rely on the fallen wood on the forest floor which, as this was the fourth course of that winter, was not very abundant without a lengthy trek which got longer and longer as the day wore on. It's amazing how much wood one can burn in a day.

That afternoon, feeling even more hungry than before, I set off with one of my team mates to search for some edible fungi in the forest. Thank heaven for those periods in the classroom. At least we had a rough idea of what we were looking for. The trouble was, we didn't find any. Oh well, I thought, I might as well take a premature look at my two night lines. When you are really hungry, the difference between night and day is less obvious. Slowly, I crept up to the two pegs I had driven into the bank with their attached lines, and just as slowly I felt for any tension on the first. To my utter astonishment and delight, there was something on the hook. Abandoning my caution, I pulled in the line as fast as I could and low and behold there on the hook was a fat little river run brown trout of about one and a half pounds weight. Still unable to believe my luck, I feverishly retrieved the second line and sure enough, there was a second, slightly smaller member of the same species. I took them both back up the hill to show them with much delight and in a supreme air of nonchalance, to Geordie. I think it was the only time I actually saw him 'mega-miffed.' He hardly spoke to me for the rest of the course. The team, however, set to in preparing the most basic, yet probably the most tasty trout stew I have ever had the pleasure to sample. I think we were the only team to actually have eaten anything other than glucose sweets for at least twenty four hours. We went to bed that night well chuffed. The following morning the youngest member of our team complained of stomach pains. Feeling sure that my trout were in someway to blame, I felt awful. However our resident Doctor, who was also one of the students, diagnosed his problem as appendicitis, so he was packed off to the nearest German Krankenhaus for its immediate removal. We all felt that it was just a ploy to get out of the next phase of the exercise which was Escape and Evasion.

That lunch time, one of the instructors, not Geordie who was still sulking over the trout, appeared with a wicker basket from which, like the proverbial magician, he proceeded to produce one live rabbit for each team. We were then given a short demonstration on how best to dispatch said rabbit to that great hutch in the sky. This to me was old hat as being country born and bred I had carried out this quick and humane method of killing for years. The rabbits were then dished out, and having offered to do the necessary to spare the sensitivities of my remaining team mate I set to preparing it for the 'pot'. Having just finished ours, I was approached by several other teams to kill, skin and joint theirs. When it came to the offal, such as the heart, liver and kidneys, there was much evidence of green faces and squeamish stomachs, so our stew eventually finished up very rich indeed. The Escape and Evasion phase, in simple terms, involved a long twenty five mile hike to attempt to reach a target at a certain time. Sounds simple doesn't it? Well what I have yet to tell you is that the Directing Staff, not to be outdone, place a few obstacles in your path. Not least of these was just about a full company of the German Army's Long Range Patrol Group, their equivalent of our Special Air Service. They had also failed to tell us that they had absolutely no intention what-

D

<u>Top: Preparing for the survival exercise. Author centre front (with gloves)</u>

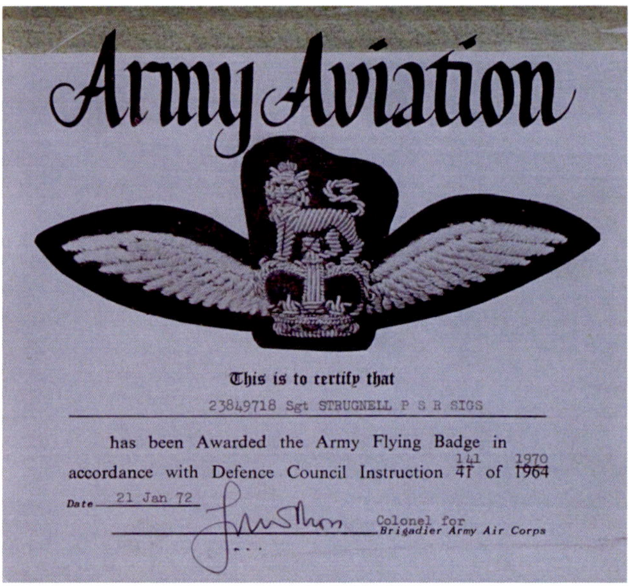

Army Aviation

This is to certify that

23849718 Sgt STRUGNELL P S R SIGS

has been Awarded the Army Flying Badge in accordance with Defence Council Instruction ~~41~~ 141 of ~~1964~~ 1970

Date 21 Jan 72

Colonel for
Brigadier Army Air Corps

Views of Berlin

Mountain Elephant in the Abedairs (Top) and a further view of the Abedair Mountains (Bottom)

Views of Mount Kenya from Nanuki

Kenya

Resupply in St Marys Mission, Rhodesia

St Marys Mission, Rhodesia

Rhodesian Ops

Views over Mount Kenya

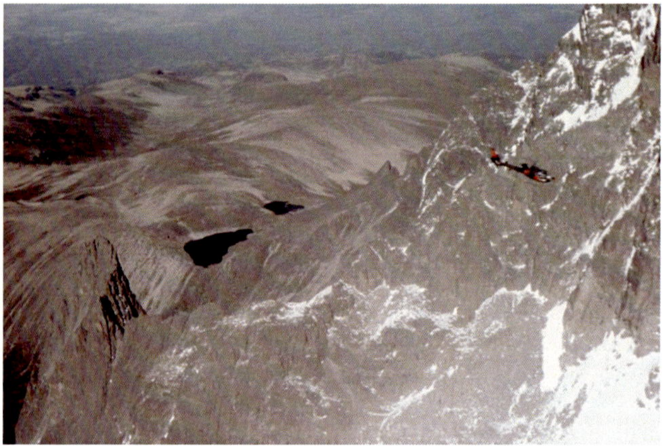

so-ever of allowing any of us to actually evade capture. I, along with most of the other members of the course, didn't think this was the most sporting of attitudes.

When we set off, the weather was turning milder, with the promise of rain in the air, which materialised at about six O'clock that evening. The elements, having thoroughly soaked our clothing, now turned really perverse. At around ten O'clock, the sky cleared to reveal a brilliant moon which was just about the last thing we hoped to see. Not content with messing up the lighting situation, the temperature plummeted to about minus twelve degrees centigrade, with the result that our clothes literally froze on our bodies. To compound the situation even further, due to the moon producing near daylight illumination, we were forced to lie up in a patch of bushes before risking the crossing of one of the major obstacles, a road through the forest only about two kilometres from the objective. That two or three hour rest period was to prove one of the most uncomfortable experiences in my entire Army career. At last the moon waned, and with what we thought was the utmost stealth, but what must have proved to the ears of the hunter force something akin to a heard of elephant on the move, we crossed the road. About fifty meters into the opposite forest belt we were captured. I didn't even hear the chaps coming. One minute we were congratulating ourselves on our success, the next – Bingo - we were well and truly clobbered.

Without a word we were tied up to a tree with our backs to the trunk and left to cool off for about half an hour, until the arrival of a Jeep to take us to the interrogation centre, blindfolded, cold and thoroughly miserable. There then followed about an hours worth of softening up routine which consisted of mainly having to successively stand, spread eagled, against a cold wall, and periods of sitting cross-legged on an equally cold metal floor with our hands on the tops of our heads, all to the accompaniment of shouted commands in Russian. By now I was showing the advance symptoms of hypothermia, and one of my guards, obviously taking into account the fact that he didn't want me to peg out before his superiors had had the chance to question me, made me stand up and led me, still blindfolded, over to what must have been a paraffin heater. The warmth that this produced was indeed heaven. However, it wasn't to last long, and very soon I was led away, stumbling, to a small room where my blindfold was removed and there, to my amazement, sat two 'Russian officers' in full uniform. I then faced several hours of interrogation which was most convincing, so much so, that after a relatively short period of time, I was firmly convinced that this was indeed for real. At the end of my 'session' it was with utter disbelief that I was informed that it was all over. I was so conditioned by this stage, that I simply didn't believe anything any more. I had, in fact, to be gently led away to enjoy the luxury of a dry change of clothing and a warm mug of tea.

Shortly after this, along with several other members of the course who were captured about the same time, we were trucked off back to the hotel for a welcome mug of hot soup accompanied by slices of dark bread. We all felt ravenous and set to with the certain knowledge that we would be able to come back for second helpings. In reality, none of us managed to finish what we had in our plates. The stomach shrinks during periods of semi-starvation, and it takes about a day and a half for ones appetite to match one's capacity. Although the experience was one I did not enjoy at the time, looking back I wouldn't have missed it for anything. At least it gave me the opportunity to test myself against the most realistic set of conditions that I am ever likely to encounter. Between February 1975 and December of that year there were the usual round of exercises, some as a

Squadron, and some as detachments supporting units of the 4th Guards Infantry Brigade, and then in early December we all started to make ready for another tour of duty in Northern Ireland. By now, knowing what to expect, it was less of a shock to the system. We all knew what was expected of us and the special flying exercises and weapon training were carried out with a new level of zeal. There were all the specialist visitors who's job it was to educate us to the current situation, both political and military, pertaining to the province at that time. The terrorists were using more sophisticated forms of bombs and mortars and we had to be as conversant with them as they themselves were. It is impossible to counter a threat of which you are ignorant. I was to be the standby pilot who would remain at base unless required to relieve any of the other pilots should that be required. Unfortunately, due to the fact that one of the other pilots did in fact have a problem which was impossible to overcome in the short term, I had to fly out on the 12th of December 1975, my birthday. This must have been a particularly difficult time for Janet, Claire and the latest addition born in April 1973, Fiona Catherine Mary, now just over 18 months old and very much a daddy's girl.

That same night I was on a Bessbrook Nitesun standby. Once more, I was back in Long Kesh in the midst of the Ulster troubles. It was only about a month later that our OC, Major David Hicks, was killed trying to cross a pylon line just to the north of Hillsborough in County Down. His crewman, an experienced observer, suffered multiple injuries including a broken pelvis. He was in fact lucky to escape with his life. It was a blessing that the aircraft had not burst into flames on impact as was usually the case with the Sioux. If that had been the case, the crewman would have certainly died. Northern Ireland had claimed another innocent life. The biggest tragedy, however, was that it was a needless death that could almost certainly been avoided had the pilot displayed a degree of captaincy. The replacement officer sent out to command the Squadron in this difficult period was Major Peter Wood, who proved a most able OC and who had everyone's utmost respect as an officer and a gentleman. It was about this time that I had yet another narrow squeak. I was on a Bessbrook Nitesun standby, and we had been called out to a suspected incident between Crossmaglen and Cullyhanna. It was a cold starlit night and there had been a report of five gunmen seen near a derelict house in a sparsely populated area near Silverbridge, moving westwards towards the border. I took off with my observer to illuminate the area for a number of patrols who were in the area. We found the group of suspects and put the light on them, which caused a bit of consternation among their number, and they ran into the derelict farm complex. We continued to illuminate the scene for the ground troops who, after a short time, came under fire. They returned fire with a GPMG (general purpose machine gun), firing tracer ammunition. I was somewhat alarmed to see that the rounds were ricocheting off the sloping slate roof of a cellar entrance and coming straight up at me. There were a series of sharp cracks as the rounds went past, and through, the rotor disc and it didn't take long for me to scream a few choice comments at the ground patrol to cease firing. I shudder to think what a tracer round in a half empty fuel tank, containing 145 octane Avgas, could have done but I expect they would have seen the resultant fireball in Belfast. There is not much more to add about that tour, it seemed to be a mirror image of the previous one. The sorties were about the same and the other details were so similar to the last tour that I will not bore the reader with what would be just pure repetition. March 29th saw me once more on a Hercules transport bound for Gutersloh in Germany and a much needed spot of leave at the conclusion of my second tour of duty in Ulster.

Chapter 5.

The City Of Courage.

Once more, on return from leave, there started the usual round of exercises here, there and everywhere. Then in April, I learnt that I was to be posted to 7 Flight AAC in West Berlin. Oh joy of joys. This was considered to be one of the best postings in the world and I was determined to make the most of it. My posting was to be effective on the 16th of June, right in the middle of the summer. There was much work to be done. Special documents needed to be applied for to enable me to travel through the autobahn corridor from Helmstedt to Marienborn in West Berlin. Janet and the children were to fly in once we had a quarter allocated. The 16th of June dawned bright and sunny. I said my temporary farewells to the family and set off up the autobahn past Hannover to Helmstedt. Many years before, I had worked at Helmstedt in my days with Royal Signals, so at least I new part of the score. Having checked in and had my documents verified, I was once more on the road, but this time in East Germany. It is a strange feeling to be travelling in what is to all intents and purposes an alien country. The autobahn in the east was atrocious. There were pot holes in the road surface, some as deep as a foot or more and one had to be ever alert of the possibility of buggering up your suspension in one of these mini coal mines. It was with a great feeling of satisfaction that at last the Soviet checkpoint at Marienborn loomed into sight, with its watch-towers and searchlights. It never ceases to amaze me that the Soviets can convince their subjects that the wall is necessary to keep us out. You only have to see the arrangement of the fortifications at the border to see that this is a blatant lie. I will at least say that on all the occasions I travelled through this checkpoint, the Soviet troops, while not always too quick to process your documents, were always very polite and correct. They were not too averse to the occasional bit of illegal trading either. It was amazing what a Ronson gas lighter could obtain in the way of Russian military clothing. Fur hats, belts and all sorts of badges were obviously not in that short supply that quite a number of these items ended up in the collections of the decadent forces of the capitalist west. The penalties for them, if caught would, I imagine have been horrendous. Enough said. Berlin is the most amazing of cities. It is cosmopolitan in the extreme. Before my arrival, I had always imagined it to be a rather claustrophobic place, surrounded as it is by a huge and ugly concrete wall. Unless you actually go looking for this monstrous obscenity of Soviet hypocrisy it could evade you for days on end. For me, however, it was not so easy to miss the wall. RAF Gatow, the base of 7 Flight, lies right up against it on the western edge of the city limits.

It is a standing rule that new pilots, on arrival in west Berlin, take the guided tour, organised by HQ Berlin, and visit the East. There is a very sound philosophy behind this ruling, in that any new pilot arriving in the city is very soon going to be the object of a lot of attention from the East Germans and the Soviet authorities. To save a lot of, what could be, unpleasantness, it is far better to take the bull by the horns and openly display the new arrivals to all those who might be interested. When visiting the east of the city, all military personnel must wear uniform, so there is never any doubt as to who is who and who does what. I remember well the amount of interest my light blue beret caused as I crossed through Check Point Charlie into East Berlin. There seemed to be cameras in every observation tower and kiosk as we passed through. As we drove around the city, there always seemed to be either a black Wartburg or a Zill following us. Eventually we got to Treptow Soviet war cemetery, where we stopped and all got out both to admire the splendid memorial to the 50,000 soviet soldiers who died in the liberation of the city, and to pay our respects. A military cemetery is a military cemetery, no matter who the soldiers buried there. It was an even more sobering experience to know that whenever I looked over my shoulder, there was always someone who self-consciously looked away and examined a memorial stone or the like. Ah well, it was, as the authorities said, better to get it out of their systems early rather than later. I think the most striking point that meets the eye of the new visitor to the east, is the fact that as you get further from the wall into the city on their side, more and more of the landscape is as it must have been left at the end of the war. Great tracts of bomb damaged buildings still as yet unrepaired, with roads that are in a similar condition. It is only near the wall that the new modern edifices of glass, steel and concrete have sprung up. The East German authorities have gone to great pains to restore the damage inflicted by the ravages of war within a mile or so of the wall, but outside that zone, it is like being transported back forty years or so. One of the most amazing feats of restoration is being carried out on the cathedral, which was almost totally destroyed during the bombing of the last great war, and is now rising again from the ashes and the rubble to its former splendour. The East German authorities must be spending a fortune on the work, just so it can be, once more a tourist attraction. The cathedral contains the tombs of the entire Hohenzollen royal family. Another strange sight is the Ost Hauptbarnhoff, the main railway station of the old German capital. In its heyday, one could catch a train here to almost any corner of Europe, now only the facade remains, and it is only from the air that you can see the ghosts of the old rail network weaving out of what was once one of the busiest stations on the continent, serving every major city of Europe.

Dominating the entire landscape of both East and West Berlin, stands the second tallest man made structure in the world, the

East Berlin TV tower. It soars above the divided city in splendour and grace. It is a copy of the Canadian National TV tower in Toronto. The architect, a west European, had the last laugh though. Near the top of the tower, is a glass globe containing a restaurant and offices, and when he designed the frames for the panes of glass each pane is faceted slightly out of true, with the effect that on a sunny day, no matter where you stand, in east or west, you will see the sign of a cross on the glass. As East Germany is an agnostic state, this causes a lot of consternation among officials on their side of the wall. They have tried all sorts of remedies to eradicate the phenomena like using a spray on coating to give the glass a matt surface, but the wind and rain stripped it off in days, they even had it covered by PVC sheeting but that suffered the same fate. It would appear that short of pulling down one of their proudest contemporary buildings, they will just have to grin and bear it. I must say that the view from the restaurant, which revolves once every twenty minutes is, on a clear day, breathtaking. Berlin is truly an amazing city. It consists of equal thirds of forest, water and built up areas. The third that consists of water is made up of grand lakes and rivers but also one of the most important junctions in the canal systems of the whole of Europe. Barges (some as big as five to six thousand tonnes) are seen from such counties of origin as Germany, Poland, Holland, France, Hungary and Czechoslovakia. All these inland ships pass through both East and West Berlin in the course of their travels to the far flung reaches of commerce. Often barges, particularly from Poland were guilty of discharging oil and fuel residues into the waters of West Berlin, and one of the jobs we were given was to follow the slick and report the name of the culprit to the West Berlin Water Police. If caught the skipper could expect to receive a hefty fine and could be detained in West Berlin for a considerable period of time until that fine were paid. The city derives nearly all its water supply from its internal reserves in the form of these waterways and obviously pollution of this kind posed a serious threat.

We worked in close co-operation with a number of the civil authorities in the city including the Wassershutzpolitzie, Berlinshutzpolitzie and the fire service. The latter was constantly troubled by fire raisers in the vast tracts of forest within the city boundaries during the long, hot, dry summer months. We would be quite busy if smoke were reported from the Grunewald or Spandau forest. Sometimes these fire raisers would start several fires spread over a large area within a few minutes of each other and the fire brigade would have to utilise nearly all their resources to cope with the problem.

Gatow, as I previously mentioned, lay in the west of the city. A large military airfield which was used for the arrival of British military and civil aircraft from the zone, as we called the rest of West Germany. Of course it was also the home of 7 flight Army Air Corps, a small and tightly knit community of some twenty two people all working towards the same aim of maintaining the integrity of this divided city. Our work, mostly classified, was aimed at the gathering and updating of intelligence information about the build up, movement and constitution of East German and Soviet units based in East Berlin. Another major task was to keep an eye on the constant improvements the East Germans were making to the wall itself. This is a wall in name only, and consists of a whole series of obstacles to deter any but the most determined attempt at escape from the East to the West. Behind the bare face of the wall, as viewed from our side, stretches an area of some fifty to two hundred meters of additional obstacles. These include ditches, trip wires connected to lethal explosive devices, mined strips of raked soil and, just for good measure, free running guard dogs restrained only by a chain running along a length of cable thus enabling each dog to cover the maximum amount of ground without the risk of it finishing up in one of the minefields. As if this were not enough, every five to six hundred meters or so there would be a tower manned by East German Border Guards with machine guns and searchlights, just for good measure. Despite these formidable 'defences' to stop the escape of the free minded, a considerable number of East Germans still make it to the west. Long may it remain so. Of course, not all those purporting to be genuine refugees are all they appear to be, and it is not unknown for the East Germans to plant the odd intelligence agent among these escapees. We always had strict orders to distract the attention of the border guards if we witnessed an attempt at escape, without endangering the aircraft or ourselves. I must admit, this only concerned me on one occasion, when a father and son made their bid for freedom on the northern edge of the Spandau forest. They were two of the successful ones.

Don't think for one moment that it was all work. The social life in Berlin among the British and German civilian communities is, to put not too fine a point on it, hectic. The summer would witness a never-ending round of barbecues and parties. There was so much to do and, in reality, so little time to do it all in. There is, as far as I know, no activity that one cannot pursue in Berlin. Whether your taste is music, sport, arts, or just lazing around, you can do it all in this amazing city. One of the jewels in the crown of the city is the Olympic stadium, which actually forms part of the Headquarters British Forces Berlin complex. Built for the 1936 Olympics, it has to be one of the best military stadiums in use today. Beside the stadium, stands the Maifeld. This is the large and very impressive grass parade ground where, during the war, Hitler used to review his followers. Now it is used once a year for the Sovereign's Birthday Parade. It is in its own way every bit as impressive as Horse Guards Parade.

Life for me in this posting was, I think, the most idyllic of my whole Army career. As a keen sailor, I very soon after my arrival enrolled in the British Berlin Yacht Club, which was literally just across the road from the main gate at RAF Gatow. I spent many pleasant hours sailing on the Havel Lake. This is so large that it seems to generate its own weather systems. I have frequently seen three to four foot waves created by sudden squalls which could knock the unwary helmsman flat in no time at all. We had a fleet of Olympic class 470s and about ten or so Laser dinghies. The competition was fearsome and the socialising equally savage. The local beer, Shultheiss, made in Spandau, had a kick like a mule. No-one went anywhere without at least a couple of six packs of 'Shultie' in the boot of their car. I think the club had almost as many social members as sailing members. Along with the 470s and Lasers, there were also a couple of Randmeer day boats, big enough to take the whole family out for the day and a picnic on the lake. This was always a treat for Janet and the children and gave us time to get away from the hurly burly of the club social scene. It was nice to just be on our own from time to time.

There were plenty of other activities to occupy our attention as well as sailing. As I previously mentioned, whatever you desired in Berlin was there for the taking. Another of my great passions is music or, to be more precise, classical music. There was the Berlin Philharmonic to be heard under the direction of the late Herbert Von Karajan in the immense concert hall near the wall on the eastern side of the Tiergarten. Over in the East was the Staats Opera, the German state Opera, and one of the pleasures of going was the fact that we had to go in uniform and that, at night and because it was 'dress,' meant Mess Kit. Imagine the scene. Members of the allied forces, French, American and British, all in their various forms and brilliant colours of Mess Dress filling the circle and stalls in a glittering array of colour. It must have been like Covent Garden during the Napoleonic wars. Scarlets, blues, golds and silver and black gathered together in a kaleidoscope of colour and pageantry. And that was on the auditorium side of the stage. Add to that some of the richest and most lavish performances performed in what must be one of the most impressive settings in the world, and you have an evening out at the Staats Opera. I only went three times but each of those occasions is still a vivid print in my mind.

In truth, my taste in music is broader than just the classics. I also enjoy jazz, both modern and traditional. Every Sunday, in one of the disused stations of the old overhead tram system, is held a flea market. It all takes place inside some of the old carriages, and in the end one is a cafe, with lively and very noisy trad. jazz. There was something almost decadent about spending a Sunday afternoon with a glass of good beer and the best of impromptu music. With so many military units in the city, there were always military band concerts to be heard.

Apart from music, there were so many sights to be seen that it would, in truth, probably take the best part of two or three years to take in everything. West Berlin is dissected by the main east/west highway of the Heer Strasse, an impressive road which runs from the west of the city right up to the city centre, changing its name to Kaiserdamm to sweep past the Olympic stadium and on into Cornelius Platz, then once more a name change to Bismarck Strasse as far as the Berlin Hilton Hotel. Here it broadens even further, and with another change of name becomes The Seventeenth of June strasse to sweep right up the very portals of the Brandenburg Gate, that most famous of symbols that demonstrates both freedom and oppression. The chariot and four horses were taken down during the war, presumably for safe keeping, but were then sunk at the bottom of the Havel lake, only to be rediscovered after the war and replaced to their original position atop the centre columns of the gate. The tragedy is that the gate itself is in the East, and because of its proximity to the wall is unapproachable from either east or west. We probably got a better view of it than any one else, as we were allowed to fly right up to the wall from the west. We were not, however, allowed to overfly the wall itself. To have done so would have caused a very major diplomatic row and the prompt removal of the culprit from the city.

There are two major sights worthy of note just off the 17th Juni Strasse, one is the Congress Halle, fondly known by the west Berliners as the 'pregnant oyster,' and nearer the Brandenburg Gate there is the Russian War Memorial. This is a rather impressive affair with a classical designed monument, flanked by two Joseph Stalin tanks each set on a concrete ramp. The memorial is manned twenty-four hours a day by Russian soldiers. It is one of only two places where Russian soldiers have free access to west Berlin. There used to be three, but now that Spandau Prison is no more that is one foothold that the Russians have lost.

Half way along the 17th Juni Strasse, in the centre of a large circular 'platze,' stands the Sieges Saule. A tall column, taller than Nelsons' Column in London, on the top of which stands the gilded figure of a winged lady, bearing aloft the tribune and laurels of the victor. It commemorates the victory over Napoleon and used to stand in front of the Reichstag building, a little way to the north-east. It was moved just before the war to its present position. Surrounding this monument is the Tiergarten with its many ornamental parks and gardens. This used to be the area in which all the major embassies had their splendid buildings. Many of these buildings still remain, but not as embassies. To the north-east of the Sieges Saule stretches the ultra modern, and to my mind, rather ugly Hansa Quarter. This was built as the

Berlin entry for the international design exhibition called Expo 76. Each building was designed by a different architect, and believe me, it shows! As we move further westwards we come to the city centre itself, dominated by the Kaiser Wilhelm Memorial Church. All that remains of the original church is the tower and the lower half of the spire. The rest was flattened during the bombing, and in memory of the war a new church was built in the shape of an octagon and glazed throughout with Blue Chartres Glass, a gift from the people of that French city. When lit from inside, the colours in the glass windows are breathtaking. Running south-west from the memorial church is the heart of Berlin, the Kurfurstendamm. This is Berlin's equivalent of Bond street, Regent street and Oxford street all rolled into one. It is the commercial and social hub of the city. At its eastern end stands the famous Kranzlers coffee house, where anyone who is anyone goes to both see and be seen. There are three floors and the coffee and service get dearer the higher you climb. There must be a moral in there somewhere.

Running north/south, from the checkpoint at Marienborn, runs the great motorway called the Avus. Twice a year the Berliners hold a motor racing meeting on the Avus, and very hairy it is too. Before the war, the German Grand Prix was staged here on more than one occasion. This great arterial route runs right up to the Funkturm, looking like a mini Eiffel Tower. It was from here that Lord Haw Haws' infamous transmissions were beamed to England. Just behind the Funkturm stands the Berlin Exhibition Centre with a modern complex of halls and gardens. Behind that stands the largest hall in Berlin, and one of the largest in Europe, the Deutschland Halle. This is so large that in the British Military Tattoo of 1976, two Sioux helicopters were flown inside at rehearsal. In fact only one aircraft was used in the performances due to the fact that the rotor down wash caused havoc with the overhead suspended lights and speakers. It was therefore considered safer to fly only one aircraft. The last person to fly inside the Halle was Hanna Reich in one of Germanys' early pioneering helicopters, some 35 years before.

To the north of the Heerstrasse lies the French Sector. This centres around the Tegel Airport and the surrounding districts and the eastern edge of the Spandau forest. In the east it stretches down to the Shloss Charlottenburg, the old royal palace, and the Turkish district of the city. I sometimes feel that the French didn't get the best of deals when the city was divided up by the allies at the end of the war. To the south-east of the Havel, is the American sector. This consists of most of the Grunewald forest and, predominantly, the district of Darhlem. One of the most advantageous benefits of having the Americans literally half an hours drive away was that we were permitted to use the American PX or post exchange. This was like a large supermarket packed with the full range of American consumer goods. It knocked spots of the NAAFI. The only problem was that purchases had to be made in US dollars which one bought at the door, so to speak, but if you were left with any over at the end of the spree, the exchange rate to turn your change back into German marks was swingeing to say the least.

The flying side of my work in Berlin was strange in the extreme. When I first started flying, the golden rule was to never, if it could possibly be avoided, overfly a built up area such as a town or city. Now I was being asked to do this over a very large city, and for considerably long periods of time. It is indeed a strange feeling. On the plus side, in the event of an emergency such as an engine failure, there were plenty of the skyscraper blocks which had strengthened roofs, which it was possible to put down onto in such a situation.

Pilots in Berlin do not only have to be experts on the composition and equipment of the Warsaw Pact units which are stationed in East Berlin, they also had to be a combination of taxi driver and tour guide. Being the place it is, and having so much to see in it, Berlin is like a honey pot to the 'brass' in the zone and indeed in the UK. Nearly every day someone would visit the city and they of course would have to be shown round in the sort of style that only the Army Air Corps could offer. They never knew it, but there were three classes of tour, the 45 minute, the 1 hour and the top of the range one and a half hour all in trip. Of course the eligibility for each class of tour depended very much on rank or what they could do for us as a unit. Throughout these trips one would be doing a non-stop commentary on the sights worthy of note. Two of the one and a half hour jobbies, in one day, and you could end up with no voice left. There were also visits from various organisations in the UK who came over to either give pleasure to the handicapped or the underprivileged. These were as much a joy to us as they were to them. We always went to it with a gusto otherwise never seen, for such organisations as the Across Trust. They would arrive in the city with their enormous and beautifully equipped ambulance coach, with probably around 15 to 20 mentally and physically handicapped patients, to be entertained by each and every unit in the Berlin Brigade. Such visits would need to last a week, just to enable them to visit everyone before leaving. We always used to lay on a couple of static aircraft and a 'handling demonstration,' just another euphemism for a flying display.

One of the most interesting people that I had the pleasure to fly over the city was the Time Life photographer, Dan Budnick, while he was involved with doing the photographs for the volume concerning Berlin in a series that publisher did on cities of the world. He was a charming man who, as it was wintertime, had the discomfort of filming out of the right hand side of a Sioux, with the door off, and in the middle of a snow storm. He was absolutely frozen when we eventually got back to Gatow. Not once had he complained, all through the flight. Talking of snow, skiing was another pursuit that could be followed in Berlin in the winter. When the city was cleared of rubble after the war, that same rubble had to be put somewhere. The ever resourceful Berliners decided to build a man-made mountain beside the Heerstrasse, and called it Teufelsburg, devils hill. This is over six hundred feet high and has two ski slopes, complete with lifts. This is the highest piece of ground in the city, the rest being an indigenous part of the great north German plain. When there was plenty of snow, the slopes would be as packed as the top alpine resort in mid season.

Just as in everything else, in terms of climate, Berlin is a city of extremes. The summers would see temperatures in the upper nineties or lower hundreds, and the winters would plunge to a numbing minus twenty to thirty centigrade. The winds were icy, there being nothing to check the sweep of the weather all the way across from the Siberian Steppes. The hot summers would bring their own benefits, in the form of naturism. With so many skyscrapers and small lakes there were plenty of places for nude sunbathing and I think we found just about all of them, much to the annoyance of the naturists. One of the most difficult sorties of my entire flying career was flown in Berlin. I had been tasked to fly a photo sortie with the object of taking a picture of the entire city in one frame. Remember that Berlin covered some six hundred square kilometres and imagine the height required to encompass such a task. We decided, by trigonometry, that an altitude of about ten thousand feet would be required. This posed several problems in itself. Firstly it was late May, and the weather was already pretty hot, and secondly, to manage a vertical shot, the photographer would have to be strapped into a

Stokes Litter (a kind of framework stretcher), face downwards, with the camera strapped under him. The maximum operational ceiling of the Sioux was 13,600 feet density altitude, and with the warm surface temperature, this meant that 10,000 feet above ground level would equate to about 13,000 feet density altitude. Well, not to be daunted, I obtained the necessary clearances to fly a sortie over the city at that altitude, briefed the photographer, Sgt Netherwood, and on 23rd May we had the all clear to go from the relevant authorities. I don't know who was more scared at the prospect, John Netherwood or me. He strapped into the litter, and we took off for what was to prove to be the most hairy trip I have ever flown. We climbed for what seemed hours but was in fact about twenty minutes, and eventually arrived at flight level 100 (10,000 feet on a standard altimeter pressure setting of 29.92 inches of mercury). I have never been so terrified in all my life. Remember that the Sioux had a great big Plexiglas bubble for a canopy and only cruised at that altitude at about 45 Kt's. It was like sitting on the top of a 10,000 foot tall flag pole. After about two or three minutes taking photographs in an outside air temperature of about minus 10 degrees centigrade, which necessitated full selection of Carb. Heat, and suffering from severe vertigo, we came down a bloody site quicker than we went up. My bum was twitching for a week after that particular trip. I certainly don't ever want to repeat the experience. I have flown higher than that since but not in a Sioux and certainly not above flat country. Mind you, I think the resultant photograph was worth the change of underwear. Of all the postings I have ever been in, I think that the challenge of flying in West Berlin offered me the most satisfaction. It is very hard to describe the degree of skill and concentration that is required when constantly flying over an enormous built up area. It is totally alien to everything that is both taught and natural. To operate in such a manner in any other theatre of operation,

supported by the Army Air Corps, other than Hong Kong, would bring an instant rebuke and probably a spell of 'grounding.'
In all, I spent just over a year in Berlin, and thoroughly enjoyed it. Then, in 1977 I was posted back to the UK to Topcliffe, in North Yorkshire. We were to leave just before Her Majesty the Queen's jubilee birthday parade on the Maifeld. That was my one and only disappointment in Berlin. We left this enchanting and cosmopolitan city on 8th June 1977. It was, indeed, with deep regret, that we drove for the final time down the corridor to Helmstedt and the zone. It was a longer than usual journey, or so it seemed, to the Hook of Holland, that summers day. One day, perhaps, I will get the opportunity to return to that most alluring of cities that I grew to know so well, and love, in that short period of time allowed to me.

Chapter 6.

From James Herriot to Livingstone and beyond.

After a spot of disembarkation leave, there not being a quarter available yet, I travelled up to North Yorkshire alone, not knowing quite what to expect. It was a long time since I had been in this part of the world. My courses at Catterick had been my last time spent in North Yorkshire, and I had forgotten what a picturesque part of the world it was. Gone were the memories of clear, laughing rivers with gravel beds, the home of brown trout. Lost, the recollection of the wide open expanses of the open moors and the beauty of the dales. All these memories were to come flooding back very quickly as, once more, I enjoyed the magic of this most beautiful of the Ridings.

Topcliffe, only a small village, lies just south of the market town of Thirsk, under the splendour of the towering mass of Sutton Bank, the western edge of the North Yorkshire Moors national park. The camp itself was between the village and Thirsk. At one time an RAF airfield, it was now the home of 1st. Regiment Royal Horse Artillery, and of course, of more interest to me, 666 Squadron, Army Air Corps. The squadron was located in one of the hangars adjacent to the airfield and, as Topcliffe was still used by the RAF as a relief landing ground for the central flying school just up the A1 at Leeming, we had the added luxury of daytime air traffic control provided by them. This meant of course that we received a full air traffic service to a very high standard. Topcliffe was, in fact, one of four stations within a small radius which all came under the overall control of RAF Leeming to the north and RAF Linton on Ouse to the south. This could create its own problems, especially if flying was intensive from both these stations. As long as we remained low level however, everyone was very tolerant towards us. To the east, over the North Moors, was a low flying area, and to the west another, over the vast expanse of the Pennines. All these splendid amenities were hitherto unknown to someone who was simply used to being able to fly just about anywhere without hindrance. Now all flights into either of these low flying areas had to be booked with the relevant controlling authorities.

666 Squadron was made up of six Sioux and six Scout helicopters, much as the formation of my first Squadron 652 at Bunde. Our role was to support the UK air portable Brigade, based in the south, but with a special responsibility to support all those units north of the wash and right into Scotland. A massive area of operation, which frequently led to detachments away from base for several days at a time. We, of course, also had a special responsibility to support Headquarters North-Eastern District based at York. I had, as previously mentioned, arrived at Topcliffe in mid summer and there is no better way of seeing this part of the world than at the height of the warm weather. In the vale of York, around the valley of the river Ouse, was the rich arable farmland that makes this area so prosperous, and over the higher ground to east and west were the smaller hill farms that produce such fine sheep and cattle. One can see at a glance why James Herriot, or Alfred White, to give him his proper name, still has his veterinary practice in Thirsk to this day, and why he writes so profusely about his beloved area. He has probably been responsible for bringing the beauty of this part of the world into the homes of more people than any one else alive. His portrayal of the Yorkshire people is both just and accurate. They are indeed a warm hearted and at times eccentric race, viewing life in a way which the average southerner finds hard to comprehend. The pace of life is so much slower here. Gone is

the hustle and bustle of the energetic existence as practiced south of what they refer to as God's country. I think I know exactly what they mean.

Within a couple of weeks of my arrival at Topcliffe, I was off on an exercise in the west of Scotland, actually based at Invergarry, in support of the Junior Leaders Regiment Royal Engineers. They were then commanded by the legendary explorer Lt. Col. John Blashford-Snell. It was to be the start of a fairly long association with this much respected man, who was to go on to be the founder and inspiration of the scheme to develop character in youngsters, through the organisations called Operations Drake and Raleigh.

This particular exercise was in the form of adventurous training among the mountains and loughs of the western highlands. It involved flying over some of the most remote and beautiful country imaginable. The Junior Leaders were both resourceful and determined, and how else could it be under the leadership of such a man as 'Blashers.' He was a strict disciplinarian, fair, but with a driving force that had to be seen to be believed. I was to fly him quite a lot over the two weeks that the exercise lasted, and came to know and respect the man enormously. The weather was hot and sunny, with the occasional summer storm to clear the air, and it was with a genuine feeling of regret that I returned to base. I could have stayed up there for a lot longer enjoying both the country and Col. John's accounts of far off distant lands. Back at Topcliffe, life resumed the same round of flying training and ferry work right through the summer. As a family we had the opportunity to explore the countryside around us and managed to visit a variety of sites of interest, such as the ruined abbeys at Bylands, Rivoux and Fountains, all of which were within easy striking distance of Thirsk. Coupled with these trips there were also visits to the Dales at weekends, where the picnic basket would come out and everyone would enjoy the relaxation of savouring the open air. One of our favourite trips, which was repeated several times, was to the magnificent country of Wensleydale, always with the reward of a farm produced cheese for a souvenir. Alas, these farm made cheeses are no longer available due to the regulations of the Common Market. All Wensleydale cheese now comes through centralised outlets. The whole of the dale is dotted with little spots, normally unseen by the passing tourist, which evoke a strong sense of the 'feel' of the county and its people. Little by-roads that lead to the edge of a wood or large pasture reveal sights that are unforgettable. Summer turned into autumn with its associated hues of red and gold, and eventually into our first taste of a North Yorkshire winter. Bleak and cold with a damp ferocity that at times was almost unbearable. That first winter, for us, was the worst we experienced in the three years that we were at Topcliffe. There was plenty of snow and frosty nights to contend with and shopping trips to the nearby town of Thirsk became mini expeditions. There was plenty of work on the flying side as well, for this was the period of the firemen's strike and we were heavily committed to supporting the Army units who were drafted in with their 'Green Goddess' machines to provide at least a basic degree of cover for the civilian population. Most of my time during this period was spent at Hull, supporting the crews from 1st Regiment, Royal Horse Artillery, who manned that particular area. Although I sympathised with the regular Firemen's demands, I could not come to terms with their methods. I know for certain that it cost the lives of at least six soldiers, only partly trained, who were trying to protect the public as best they could. I shall always feel that their lives were the price for the subsequent pay rise the Firemen eventually received.

At the end of August 1977, I was given the chance to go to Cyprus for an attachment to 16 Flight AAC. for a month. This was an opportunity not to be missed and I jumped at the chance. I had never been to Cyprus before and relished the thought of visiting this enchanting Mediterranean island. The Flight was based in the Eastern Sovereign Base Area (SBA) at Dakehlia, just north of the town of Larnaca with its civilian airport. It was a truly marvellous experience and one that I certainly would not have missed for anything. I think one of the most memorable trips I did in my spare time was a visit to the monastery of Stavrovouni, sitting like some castle in the sky, atop a pinnacle of rock, some 700 meters high, on the eastern edge of the Trudos Mountain range. I don't think I have ever experienced such a deep feeling of peace and tranquillity as I did while in that beautiful monastic house perched between heaven and earth. The Monastery of Stavrovouni was allegedly built on the orders of St. Helen on her way back to Greece in 327 - 330 A.D. after she was returning from Jerusalem after discovering the Holy Cross of Christ. At the present location of the Monastery there was a heathen altar dedicated to the goddess Aphrodite. Women were not permitted to approach and legends said that devils dwelt in it. St. Helen had noticed this altar while she was at sea and after she had learned what it was she said that she would change it into a church of God. Tradition reckons it to be the oldest monastery in Cyprus.

Of course, as well as the work there was plenty of time to play and the waters around Cyprus are some of the best in the Mediterranean for swimming and diving. I availed myself of its facilities as often as I could. On the flying side the experience was equally rewarding and, having obtained my theatre acceptance check, I set to with a will to discover as much of the island as I was able to in just one short month. One of the biggest bonuses for me was the fact that there was a very active gliding club operating out of a disused airfield on the northern edge of the Dakehlia SBA, which I joined as a temporary member. My weekends and Wednesday evenings were thus taken up to the full. After a successful and very enjoyable weekends gliding, all the members would retire to a very pleasant and picturesque restaurant just outside Larnaca, where we would partake of the best Mezze on the Island. This would consist of at least fifteen, and sometimes as many as eighteen dishes, all locally caught or killed. The veranda of the establishment overhung the sea and all the fish dishes came straight from 'la mare' to the kitchen. Red mullet, crayfish, octopus, squid and many other delicacies were offered to the lucky diners as fresh and well prepared as one could ever wish for. The whole meal was washed down with copious amounts of the local wines. It was, indeed, a very civilised way to end a perfect weekends flying in superb style. Larnaca was also the site of all the local skills and trades, especially leather work, and I was able to have two pairs of shoes made for me for the unbelievable price of about twenty-five pounds. The time simply galloped by and alas it was all too soon when I had to pack my bags and return to Topcliffe and the family.

666 Squadron was the last of the Army's units to be equipped with Siouxs, all the remaining Squadrons having already been equipped with the new Anglo/French designed Gazelle helicopter built under licence by Westland Helicopters at Yeovil and Weston-Super-Mare. At last, in March 1978, we were to join the rest of the Corps and convert to the Gazelle. On the 24th of February we had a farewell flypast at Topcliffe and then flew our Siouxs down to Wroughton in Wiltshire for the last time. It was a sad farewell to an aircraft that had served the British Army for many years and to very good effect.

After this we all went down to Middle Wallop to convert onto the new type. This conversion lasted six weeks and the difference between the Sioux and the Gazelle was akin to the difference between a Ford Cortina and a Ferrari. The French

design was very manoeuvrable, very comfortable and compact, and very, very, fast. It represented the difference between a first generation helicopter and a third or fourth generation design. And it showed. Gone were the days of trogging over the countryside at 70 knots. Now we were to be covering the ground at a magnificent 120 knots. Two nautical miles every minute. I fell in love with the Gazelle almost as soon as I had got used to its incredible sensitivity. It was a pure joy to fly. It had been designed to accommodate small Frenchmen and it fitted me perfectly. I know that cannot be said for any unfortunate pilot who was over five feet ten inches tall. For them it was a different story. It proved to be rather cramped and claustrophobic. Another advantage over the Sioux was the Gazelle's ability to carry four passengers, albeit in rather confined conditions. It seemed to have almost unlimited power after the power deficiencies of the Sioux. It was as if a whole new world had opened up to us, and it was with incredible pride that at the end of the conversion course we flew our newly collected aircraft back from Wroughton to Topcliffe. It was while we were away on our conversion course that the Squadron changed its title to 655 Squadron Army Air Corps. We now had inherited a battle honour to boot. Anzio.
Once back, we had a period of consolidation on the Gazelle before we became fully operational in our new birds. Now the flight from Topcliffe to places like Edinburgh or Newcastle took half the flying time as previously taken by Sioux. At that time the Gazelle held no less than five world records for a single engined helicopter.

655 Squadron AAC, along with the resident Squadron at Netheravon in Hampshire were, as previously mentioned, used as the supporting units for nearly all the major exercises both at home and abroad. It was in 1978 that I had the opportunity to support the 2nd Battalion Grenadier Guards on one of their

battle group exercises in Kenya. This was my first visit to Africa since a short rest period spent in Mombassa in 1964, while I was serving in the Radfan war in Aden. Funnily enough, on that occasion, I went with some colleagues to climb Mount Kenya, and stayed overnight in Nanyuki which was where this particular exercise was to be based. We arrived in Nairobi at the beginning of the wet season when the veldt was looking at least a little bit green. We immediately rigged our Gazelles and as soon as all was as it should be, we took off for Nanyuki some 70 miles north of Nairobi, on the lower slopes of Mount Kenya itself. Between Nairobi and Nanyuki, the ground rises over three thousand feet as one crosses the great coffee plantations of the Kikuyu reserve. Our camp was to be situated on the edge of the Nanyuki polo club but the club itself was strictly out of bounds unless you happened to be at least a Captain, or so it seemed. Well we did not care too much as most of the members of the polo club seemed to be the most incredible snobs.

We took to Kenya with us Staff Sergeant Mick Sharpe, our Squadron QHI (qualified helicopter instructor) whose job it would be to pass us as being competent to operate in Kenya. He was later joined by Captain John Ball who was one of the most experienced QHIs from Netheravon. I think that the main reason he came out was for the 'jolly' but it was a pleasure to have him with us and to learn from his vastly superior experience. There are a lot of problems with flying a Gazelle at the sort of altitudes and in the temperatures and humidity levels of Africa, and it took us the best part of a week to come to grips with some of these potentially dangerous conditions. One of the main problems was the degraded performance caused by altitude and temperature. All control movements had to be correspondingly more smooth and gentle. It didn't take to long to get the hang of it, and as a reward we were then allowed to celebrate by actually flying up to and over the summit of Mount Kenya itself, at a height of 17,000 odd feet. At that sort of altitude even the smallest harsh control movement would result in a gentle descent. It certainly taught us to handle the aircraft with the most gentle of touches. These trips always had to be carried out in the very early morning, as after about 8:00 AM the summit would be shrouded in cloud. The view from over the top of the summit was, to say the least, breathtaking, if you will excuse the pun. (after all we were at an altitude of over 17,000 above sea level). The slopes of the mountain melted away down to the lowlands of the Nanyuki basin and then rose again about fifty miles to the west as the foothills of the Aberdare mountains bordering the great Rift Valley. That was one of the most striking things about Africa, the incredibly clear air that allowed visibility over distances hitherto unknown as far as I was concerned. Sixty miles, from a thousand feet, was an average day. A good day would allow visibility of over a hundred miles from a height of about fifteen hundred feet above ground level.

The great expanses of bush that surrounded our base at Nanyuki were teeming in game of all sorts. There were plenty of Gazelles of all types, and antelopes by the score. Zebra, Giraffe and Elephant were all regularly to be seen, and in large numbers as well. Of course there were common sightings of other animals such as Buffalo, Lion and many more. Each day was like an airborne safari. I didn't know, until I went to Africa, that there are two distinct types of African Elephant for example. The small Mountain Elephant and its much larger relative, the Plains Elephant. Both of these types were to be found near Nanyuki sitting as it did on the slopes of Mount Kenya. Also to be seen in abundance on the mountain were the beautiful black and white Collabus monkeys. These, when startled by the sound of a helicopter, would make an incredible sight as they stampeded through the tops of the jungle canopy, springing with such grace from tree to tree and all some hundred feet above the ground.

The vast majority of the plains surrounding the exercise area were much the same to look at, areas of grass and scrub acacia trees with the occasional small native village standing out like a freckle on the gold of the savannah. Standing up proud and gaunt in this scene were the Kopjes; small rocky hills isolated from each other by the scrub plain, yet high enough to be able to provide both lookout and sanctuary for numerous animals, particularly at night. All this 'sameness' made navigation particularly difficult. Every village or kopje looked like the next. It was definitely a case of believing in the planning you had already carried out, and the compass. Unless the weather was bad, which wasn't very often, it was never difficult to get home as it is a little hard to miss the largest mountain in Kenya, and the second largest Mountain in the whole of the continent of Africa. However, it is amazing how small it looks from a hundred miles away.

The exercise, called Exercise Grand Prix, was spread over a considerable area of ground, with three main company locations at Doldol, Archers Post and Gathiuru, with the Btn. HQ. back at Nanyuki. The distances were about sixty miles between the locations, all except Gathiuru, which was only about ten or so miles away from Nanyuki, on the foothills of Mt. Kenya. This particular location was used to practice the art of Jungle Warfare. By contrast, the location at Archers Post sixty miles to the north, was suitable for desert training. The contrasts were extreme. Doldol, while being near to Archers Post, was more like the countryside of Cyprus or Aden. Great gullies of red sand dotted with acacia trees and thorn bushes. Because of the deep gullies, it was considered to be the most suitable site for a live range and close quarter battle rang. Rising above the gullies in the valley bottoms were some pretty spectacularly wooded mountains. Some of these climbed to over three thousand feet above the surrounding plains. Flying in these hills was equally spectacular. As the reader can imagine, with the vast temperature changes encountered between sun-rise and sun-set, much turbulence was created, which made for some interesting flying, particularly for the unwary.

One of the most saddening trips I had to fly while in Kenya was for a local game warden who had had a report of poachers operating in his area, particularly after Elephant. One of the local tribesmen had reported seeing an Elephant Cow, obviously in distress from his description, only about two or three miles from the wardens home. Being in the area on another job, and knowing how impenetrable the area in which the animal was seen was, I volunteered to fly the warden out to see if we could find, and if possible help, the stricken beast. After only a few minutes of searching, we saw the sick Elephant trying desperately to remain on all fours by leaning against a stout tree, obviously in great distress, and quite clearly beyond all form of help other than to put her out of her misery. Having landed and cautiously approached the animal, and after giving her as good an examination as was possible, it was obvious that a dead fall spear trap had claimed another victim. The spear head had entered the right shoulder some time before, maybe weeks before, and had slowly and agonisingly worked its way down inside the right foreleg and into the foot. In simple terms, she was fast dying of blood poisoning. Jan, the warden, decided that the kindest thing to do was to end her misery and shoot her. I will never forget the expression in that poor animals eyes. It was shear gratitude. I vowed that if I ever came upon poachers after that, I would shoot them myself. Nowadays, that vow could be quite interesting, as the poachers use automatic weapons and explosive traps.

Midway through the seven week exercise we had the chance to take a 4 day break while the Battalion regrouped for the second phase. Most of the detachment decided that they would go down to the coast and visit Mombassa. The Air crew had, however, discovered a little game lodge up on an escarpment about 70 miles due north of Nanyuki, called Colcheccio. Run by Jimmy and Rose Caldwell, it provided a pleasant run down location for those tourists who had been enjoying the hurly burly of the main round of game lodges such as Kikourok Tree Tops and The Ark. The pace of life at Colcheccio was in direct contrast to the main lodges. Here one could do as little or as much as you liked. Set on the top of an escarpment overlooking the only major water hole for miles around, the subject of everyone's attention came to you. There was a wide veranda equipped with plenty of binoculars with which to sit and enjoy the game in comfort. This was where I chose to spend my spell of R and R. In the early morning I would go out riding in the bush with one of Rose's horses. There is no better way of observing the wild life than from the back of a horse. All the wild animals accept the passage of a horse where the passage of just a human would drive them all off into the dense scrub, never to be seen again. I remember, one morning, being accompanied for several hundred yards by a silver back Jackal, who showed not the slightest bit of concern about my presence. The only thing that one had to be a bit careful about was not to disturb a lone Buffalo. These are probably the most unpredictable and therefore the most dangerous animals in the bush which, when disturbed, especially if asleep, can charge in the most alarming way. The cool of the evening would be spent with whoever was staying at the lodge at the time, enjoying one of the excellent dinners devised by the Caldwells. Believe me they were wonderful hosts. After the obligatory drinks on the veranda, one would retire about ten or eleven O'clock for a deep and uninterrupted sleep until the dawn at about six in the morning. It made for a wonderfully relaxing four days. It was even better for me, as I had one of the other pilots come and pick me up when I was due to return to Nanyuki and a more normal form of life. While I was staying at Colcheccio, I met one of the Caldwell's friends, one James McLeod, who also had a little private game ranch about twenty miles away. I was invited, when in the area, to drop in and visit him some time in the future. This I did about two weeks after leaving Colcheccio, and was amazed to be met by a fully grown Cheetah who, as soon as I opened the aircraft door, jumped into the back and proceeded, much to my alarm, to lick the back of my flying helmet. The noise inside the helmet was akin to being rubbed hard with a coarse grade of sandpaper. Jimmy came out to reassure me and to introduce me to this beautiful animal. Her name was 'Puss Cat,' she was 11 months old, and she had been found as a cub by Jimmy after her mother had been killed by poachers. Because it is illegal to make any wild animal captive in Kenya, she grew up running wild about the ranch being educated by his two Rhodesian Ridgeback dogs. I'm convinced that she really thought she was a dog herself. Whenever Jimmy used to go away on business in his Cessna light aircraft, she would run along beside the plane until it took off. A Cessna lifts off in those conditions at about 55 knots (60 miles per hour). She would then mope about the place until he returned. She would hear his engine miles off, and be waiting for him at the airstrip as soon as he touched down. She was a wonderful character.

The second phase of the exercise was to prove, for me, the most exciting. By now the weather had well and truly broken and the rains were on us in earnest. When it rains on the equator (and Nanyuki was smack bang on the equator), it really rains. Not as we know rain in this country but a deluge that is hard to describe. The visibility may drop to only a hundred yards or so and it is not uncommon for about two inches or more to fall in half an hour. To stand out in it is painful, the sheer weight of water is phenomenal. Well, it was just after one of these tropical downpours that I was doing a compressor wash on the aircraft, which involved running the engine on the ground to wash off all the muck that accumulates on the 1st stage compressor blades and would otherwise impede performance. Just as I was about to shut down, I got a frantic message from the command post that there had been a snake bite incident up at Archers post. It was getting dark and not to be daunted, I radioed Archers Post to see what their weather was like. Having been assured that it was still clear up there I got the Doctor on board and, having first topped up the fuel, off we went, on top of the cloud at about 12,000 feet to pick up this chap from the north. When we arrived it was pitch black with a hole in the cloud over the top of the landing site. Archers Post is three thousand feet lower than Nanyuki and I had to spiral down for what seemed like forever, to position myself for an approach to the crossed vehicle head lamp landing aid that the company had provided for me. As soon as we landed the doctor was off like a shot to have a look at the unfortunate victim. He was, at this stage, in a coma, and the Doctor gave him a couple of injections to revive him and then we put him in the aircraft for the seventy odd mile journey back to RHQ. Twice on the way back he stopped breathing and the Doc had to drag him back to the land of the living. We had the same procedure back at base to get on the ground and within an hour of the call from up north he was safely tucked up in bed at Nanyuki. The only aid to navigation while above the cloud had been a VHF radio homing facility. Not known to be one of the most accurate methods of getting from A to B. Anyway, it had certainly worked for me. I think the whole thing had somewhat impressed the Doctor and the C.O of the Grenadier Guards. It was touch and go for the young man with the snake bite for a while but within a couple of hours he was sitting up in bed and enjoying a bit more of life once more. At any rate his recovery had saved me another journey on to Nairobi.

Before the end of the detachment, I had the chance to go, for a weekend, to the game lodge at Samburu. Situated in the north of the exercise area on the banks of the Uaso Nyiro river, it is famous for its wide variety of game and in particular its crocodiles. We arrived on the Saturday at about midday and, after a leisurely lunch, set off to explore the various tracts of land that went to make up this most varied and sometimes spectacular part of the northern rift valley. We were rewarded with splendid views of all sorts of antelope, big cats, elephant, buffalo and smaller mammals such as mongooses and a wide variety of bird species. However, the most spectacular experience was to come in the evening. Just outside the main lodge building, on the banks of the river, the owners have constructed a 'croc slide.' This consists of a muddy ramp leading from the river to the side of the lower veranda (which was surrounded by a two foot high wall). Around this slope there were a number of floodlights which, at dusk, were put on very dimly and as night fell the intensity was slowly increased. One of the native wardens would then ring a bell and lay out a quantity of bones and bits of meat at the top of the slide. We would then gather on the veranda and wait. It didn't take long for several pairs of beady eyes to appear in the river at the bottom of the slide and one by one several small crocodiles would heave themselves up the slope towards the bait. There is something very menacing about a crocodile intent on getting a free meal. They move in the purposeful way. It isn't unusual for a larger animal to attack a smaller one if the mood takes it. Suddenly we realised that all the native waiters and staff had retreated from the veranda, up the steps to the main lodge building. The word went round that this was because someone had spotted a very large crocodile making its way towards the slide. the natives called this "the black one." It was truly enormous. At least 18 feet long with a gnarled and blackened skin. It slowly made its way up the slide towards what remained of the scraps. Just to my right was a female German tourist who was operating a particularly expensive Leica camera. Just as the crocodile got to the bait, a Ginnet cat came down from above and started to pinch some of the small pieces of meat that were lying around. Quick as a flash, the crocodile swung its head over to the left and deftly gobbled up the cat. As it swung to its left its tail thrashed over to the right, striking the wall of the veranda a tremendous thump. The female German tourist dropped her camera over the wall as she did a fair impersonation of a Harrier Jump Jet. The crocodile then proceeded to eat the camera. I don't know which she was more worried about, the fright she had just received or the loss of her camera. We left Kenya on the 15th of December 1978, just in time to get home for the festive season. It had been a wonderful experience and one that, little did I know it, was to be repeated in 1980, but to a different spot on the African continent. I wasn't to get much of a break after Kenya as we were, as a squadron, preparing for yet another 4 month tour of duty in Northern Ireland. We had just two months to get up to speed for the rigours that we all knew lay ahead. This, incidentally, was to be one of the last tours to be done out of the Long Kesh location. It was also to see a meteoric advance in the technology of hunting terrorists. It was about this time that the British Army had some of its greatest triumphs over the baddies. By the end of 1979, the prisons were to be full of the scum. I suppose it was this situation of all the bad eggs in one basket, so to speak, that led to the mass breakout from the Maze prison in 1983.

The only major difference between this and previous tours was the speed at which we could complete the task in hand due to the vastly superior speed of the Gazelle. We returned to Topcliffe on the 13th June 1979 with no major mishaps to mar the time over the water.

It was at this time that I was, at last, persuaded to take the plunge and become an instructor. To this end most of the next six months or so were to be spent brushing up my knowledge and flying skill in preparation for the 13 week course at the Royal Air Force Central Flying School at Shawbury in Shropshire, which I was to attend in the following April. Topcliffe, however, had one more pleasant surprise in store for me before my departure to Shawbury. As previously mentioned, Topcliffe was one of the UK units which was responsible for maintaining a standby formation in the event of it being needed in any part of the world at short notice. This was called Operation Spearhead Standby. At the end of the year we, or at least some of us, were indeed on Spearhead standby, and as luck would have it on New Years Eve 1979, I was called abroad to Rhodesia to assist in the support of the Commonwealth Monitoring Force under the command of Lord Soames, in reality acting as a reinforcement to the Squadron from Farnborough who were already over there. What a wonderful opportunity. There was no way that I was going to miss this one. I have always been an avid reader of Wilbur Smith books and this was to be Wilbur Smith country. The land of the Matebilli. It was a strange set up when we arrived. We were based with the Rhodesian Air Force in the military side of Salisbury Airport, called New Sarum. The Rhodies were grounded for the duration of the ceasefire and were only allowed to take any part in the proceedings if that ceasefire were to be broken. Obviously they were praying for that break in the fragile situation. They had been involved in a savage bush war with both ZANLA and ZIPRA for a good many years and it, quite naturally, irked them that we were now flying the leaders of these organisations out to and back from the assembly areas. We had a big blue and white marquee erected on the civilian side of the airfield to be used as a departure and reception centre for these much disliked men. If we had landed them on the military side there is no doubt in my mind that they would have been shot on sight, such was the hatred felt towards them. The Rhodesians had flown their helicopters for all those years, protected by a bristling array of weapons. All we had to protect us was a white cross painted on the sides and the belly of the aircraft. It didn't seem to be very prudent, however there was not one incident where one of our aircraft was fired on by the PF. (Patriotic Front). The assembly areas were in effect just big campsites in the middle of the bush either geared to accept ZANLA (Zimbabwe African National Liberation Army) or ZIPRA (Zimbabwe Independent Peoples Republican Army), overseen by a force of commonwealth troops provided by Fiji, Australia, Canada and Great Britain, numbering some 1,200 in all. That the whole thing worked as well as it did right up to the elections in which Mr Mugabe was duly elected President, has got to be a tribute to the soldiers stuck out often in the middle of nowhere whose job it was to keep the peace between these highly excitable and totally unpredictable people. I know from my point of view it was a pretty unnerving experience to fly into one of these assembly areas and to have several hundred AK47 assault rifles pointed up at you with only a white cross to hide behind. It is yet another 'adrenaline' situation. I only had one real scare while I was in Rhodesia. It was on a trip, flying one of the PF leaders to an assembly area for a political rally. After about two hours on the ground, during which time the PF 'General' had consumed more whisky than was good for him, we set off to fly back to Salisbury. When we were established in the cruise at about three thousand feet above ground, the said 'gentleman' tried to convert me to his own Marxist principles. I was fairly busy at the time on the radio trying to make contact with Salisbury air traffic control and I found his political tirade rather tiring, so I turned down the volume on his intercom. He took exception to this and then proceeded to shout across the cabin at me. I asked him to "please be quiet." He, in a fit of pique, reached over to his aide, who was sat in the back seat, and removed a hand grenade from the, now trembling, aide's webbing. He then pulled the pin and held on to the lever very tightly. He had, I think, at that moment realised just what he had done. In as calm a voice as I could muster, I told him that if he let go of the lever he would be dead just a split second before me. He thought about this for a couple of seconds and then spent an agonising two or three minutes trying to replace the pin. Fortunately, he succeeded. Needless to say, I refused to ever carry this chap again. It didn't seem to do him any harm as he went on to be a minister in the new government. I expect my report was just filed in file thirteen - the dustbin.

One of my greatest pleasures was, as usual, going game watching on route to any of the locations I was visiting. Rhodesia is also rich in game but of a different variety than Kenya. Two of the most sought after species, as far as I was concerned, were the Black Rhinoceros and the Black Sable, or Orinx, which is the national symbol of the country. I saw both. The Rhino were spotted while on a recce trip along the Zambezi river and the Orinx were seen near Lake McElwain just to the Northwest of Salisbury. Speaking of the Zambezi, one of the most spectacular sights of my entire life has got to be my first view of the Kariba Dam. This massive structure lies in a deep gorge at the south-eastern tip of the Kariba lake. I was flying along the river doing a recce for PF forces coming into one of the assembly areas, when I decided to be a bit naughty and have a look at the dam itself. I entered the twisting, steep sided gorge, flying about one hundred feet above the river. After a short while the gorge became even steeper and more curvaceous and then, suddenly, as I rounded yet another bend, there it was. A massive bastion of concrete, rising majestically above the river for about four hundred feet. Suddenly, as though trying to repel my approach, one by one, the sluice outfalls were opened. One by one rods of solid water shot out from the face of the dam under tremendous pressure to break into fantails, before cascading down into the bottom of the ravine. The obvious power was awe inspiring. When all five of these huge horizontal columns of water were in full spate, I could actually hear the roar above the noise of the aircraft. Feeling very humble at witnessing such force, I gently climbed up out of the gorge and went back to the task in hand. I had witnessed all this from a distance of well over half a mile. Alas, after a short one month in this beautiful country, I was recalled to Topcliffe, our services no longer required by the other Squadron. There were only two of us and just two aircraft, who were loaded onto a Hercules transport of the RAF at Salisbury, that late January day, and I remember the feeling that maybe, God willing, I would be able to return to this land of magical contrasts. We staged back through Athens, and in the morning of our departure to good old 'Blighty' I took a taxi ride up the Acropolis to view the Parthenon in the clear morning light. I remember it was also the only time I picked up 'Med Tummy.' It was a pretty miserable trip from Athens to Brize Norton. I seemed to spend most of the time in the rear of the aircraft, where the toilet facilities were situated. Believe me, it was a very long eight hour trip.

Our arrival back at Topcliffe was greeted by a cold and frosty January day and I felt pretty miserable at the prospect of going through an English winter after the balmy warm weather of southern Africa. I now had the prospect of some real work ahead of me to prepare for my impending course at RAF Shawbury as the system ground on, to make me an instructor.

Chapter 7.

Graduation.

It was at this time that my marriage broke down and it was a blessed relief whenever I got the chance to go on detachments and exercises at various locations in the country. There were several of these, mostly for two or three days and mostly in the Otterburn area of Northumberland. All the time I was working up to the day when I would leave Topcliffe, and travel south-westwards to Shropshire and Shawbury. At last in May 1980 came the great day. Little did I know of what was to be in store for me. Up to this stage I firmly believed that I could fly. The next few weeks were to prove that theory utterly wrong.

Shawbury is the RAF central flying school for helicopter pilots and the Tri-Service helicopter instructor school. It is also responsible for the training of the forces air traffic controllers. I was to be accompanied on the course by another Army Air Corps senior NCO pilot, Sgt. Pete Arger. The remainder of the students were a mixture of RAF, Royal Navy, Royal Australian Navy and Australian Army. We were a pretty mixed bunch both in flying and social backgrounds. Incidentally, our Royal Australian Naval member was the split image of Rolf Harris, but more of that later. We were split up into pairs with whom we were to be teamed for the duration of the course. My 'stick buddy' was Flight Lt. Paul Rosentall, Royal Air Force. 'Rosie,' as he preferred to be known, and I got on like a house on fire, and we became firm friends as well as fellow students.

Our instructor, for the first part of the course at least, was Flt. Lt. John Follis, one of the true 'old and bold'. His required standard of performance was to prove to be nothing but super perfection.

As I previously mentioned, up to this stage in my flying career, I had firmly believed that I could fly. Now I was not quite so confident. In eight years of flying, one picks up a lot of non standard practices and bad habits. The first part of the first week was devoted to eradicating these problems. It felt as if our brains were being taken apart and rebuilt bit by bit. Every pure flying exercise was flown in order and each and every fault corrected. It was literally a case of back to the drawing board for most of us. Now started the really hard bit. Once more, and in the order that they appeared in the flying manual, each exercise was flown, first with John instructing us, and then with Rosie and I in turn instructing each other in the scenario of instructor and pupil, with each of us taking his turn as the instructor. So it was that we worked our way through all thirty odd exercises in the flying manual, from an introduction to the effects of controls, to formation flying. The RAF Gazelle had one refinement not normally fitted to Army aircraft. That was a Stabilisation Augmentation System, SAS for short. This was a sort of auto pilot which, once trimmed correctly, allowed a lot of the workload of actually flying the aircraft to be eased. The only problem was that, not being used to it, Pete Arger and myself, the two Army pilots were, for the first week or so, suffering from very sore thumbs from trying to continually trim the SAS instead of trimming it once and leaving it alone. The idea of the SAS was that by the use of rate giros, it would maintain whatever trim setting was put into the system at the time. This relieved the pilot of about 90% of the small control movements normally required for smooth flight. It certainly took a lot of getting used to. One interesting fact was that as it was fitted to all RAF Gazelle Mk. 2 aircraft, if it went wrong, it was considered to be an emergency and the aircraft was to be landed as soon as possible. This never ceased to amaze Pete and myself, as not having this facility fitted to our Army Gazelles, we must, in the RAF's eyes, have been flying in an emergency situation for years. It just goes to show the difference in mentality between the two services.

Frustration turned to desperation as we strove to meet the incredibly high standards expected of us. There were many times in that thirteen weeks when I firmly believed that I would not make it to the end. On top of the flying problems I was, you must remember, also going through the initial stages of a divorce. Not the most satisfactory situation to be in for such an important phase of my career. Just as on my initial flying course at Middle Wallop, we worked very hard and we played very hard. Our local course hostelry was a delightful pub on the road to Shrewsbury called the Dog in the Ditch. We referred to it less reverently as the Bitch in the Ditch. The beer was good and the company was even better. As there was a considerable amount of evening work to be completed for the next day's classroom work, we only managed to get down to the pub once, or at most twice, a week. As the reader can imagine, those occasions were an occasion for quite a bit of letting down of hair. With one exception, the course managed to ignore all rank and class barriers. The notable exception was one of the Royal Naval officers whom, it seems, could never forget his rank of Lt. RN. No names, no pack drill as the saying goes, but I'm sure if he reads this he will know who I mean. Our two Australians were great fun, and seemed to have access to an almost unlimited supply of Aussie beer (tubes) from the Australian Embassy. Time seemed to fly past in a blur of classroom lectures, presentations by members of the course and pure flying training. In the evening the whole course would assemble in the ground training school to utilise the mass of aids and equipment necessary for the production of all the training paraphernalia we needed to present our lesson to the course in the classroom.

At the half way point, we all had an individual presentation on a non flying subject, to give to the instructors and the other members of the course. This gave everyone a chance to impart some knowledge of a personal and specialised nature for the education and amusement of all. The subjects ranged from Trout fishing from yours truly, to the complex aerodynamic qualities and intricacies of how to throw a boomerang. After this latter subject, we all went outside for a practical demonstration and the chance to have a go ourselves under the careful guidance of our two Aussies. It was during the presentation by the Royal Australian Naval Lt. that the whole courses were reduced to hysterical fits of laughter. He was using an overhead projector to display some of his training aids and had inadvertently stepped into the beam of light with the result that his profile was thrown onto the screen behind him. I mentioned previously that he bore more than a striking resemblance to Rolf Harris, well here he was, Rolf in the flesh, and talking in the same dialect too! One of the technical subjects that we had to research on the flying side was the old chestnut of why a bumblebee can't fly, and why, in fact, it can. Of course the real reason he can fly is because no body told him it was aerodynamically impossible. There was so much to learn and so little time to learn it in, or so it seemed.

After the mid course check, which came in June, we had a change of instructor. We kept our pairings however, as far as our stick buddies went. Rosie and I were to have Flt. Lt. Tim Southern RAF for the remainder of the course. He was even more of a stickler for perfection than John Follis had been. Once more my chuff chart took a nose dive and I wondered if I was ever going to get that magic bit of paper at the end of the day. Well, I did manage it and on the 17th of July 1980, and after nearly 80 hours of flying at CFS(H), I qualified as a fully blown QHI. The climax of the course was still to come. This was to be a course graduation dinner in the Officers Mess. What a night it turned out to be. When you have been under enormous strain for a long period of time, you tend to let your hair down in a BIG way when the pressure is off at last. Someone, I forget who, developed a bazooka, made from beer cans, and powered by lighter fuel, which shot tennis balls at an unbelievable velocity all over the mess. This didn't go down very well with some of the other mess members not involved with our party. We started off the celebrations with a lethal cocktail, the basis of which was milk and brandy, I seem to recall and which had a kick like a mule. Then, it was decided to rig up the AOC's cutlery to black threads, connected to his chair. I know, it is all very childish, but at the time it certainly relieves the tension of thirteen weeks of very hard work. We had also rigged a couple of thunder flashes under the table to be detonated at some unknown time during dinner. We had the pleasure of a WRAF admin officer at dinner and the said thunder flashes were perilously close to her table setting. Sure enough, the cutlery jape worked a treat, to the accompaniment of stony faces and later, during the dessert, the thunder flashes went off, lifting the dining table about six inches off the ground, closely followed by the WRAF officer who, to judge by her vertical velocity, had probably left her knickers behind. At this stage in the proceedings we were advised by the AOC to 'cool it' and we all retired to the bar for some serious drinking. Course 188 had two more tricks up its sleeve however. We had managed to get hold of an old piano that was due for the scrap heap, and we decided that this would be a good prop for our finale. We dragged it out of the mess front entrance and on to the sweeping tarmac drive at the front of the building. Here we set it alight, just to see how far it would burn up before the station fire service got their act together and managed to put it out. It burnt for a long time, and in fact was pretty well demolished before the fire tender turned up to direct their jets of water on to the now smouldering embers. The unfortunate thing was that an old piano produces a lot heat when burning, and it had done a considerable amount of damage to the tar macadam drive.

The final sting in our tails was a trip to one of the old blister hangars on the side of the airfield, which was duly scaled, and the course number, 188, applied in white paint. This was still visible, incidentally, when I had to make a return trip for some reason or other some months later. All together it had been a memorable night even though we all knew that the repercussions were going to be pretty severe. The following morning brought the expected summons to appear in front of the brass. Sure enough, there had been plenty of raised eyebrows that morning when the full extent of our nights play had come to light. I was petrified. I could see all my hard work going for a ball of chalk. As it turned out, we had a great ally in the form of Sqdn. Ldr. Ross, the OC. He championed our cause with the powers above and the net result of our penance was to have to pay towards the cost of the road being patched up by the DOE, not all that expensive, and to make a contribution towards the Mess funds. I think in all it came to about thirty pounds a head. Well worth it for the nights play, was the general feeling of us all. At least we were all qualified as B2 QHIs and that, after all, was the object of the exercise. Now we were to go our own ways. Pete and I, along with our Australian Army Air Corps Lt, were destined to depart for the good old sausage machine at Middle Wallop. Life for me had gone almost a complete circle. It was to me now that the students would be looking for their succour and support. It was me now who would be responsible for the standard of the future generations of Army pilots. It was me who would have to show the highest standards of flying skill and discipline without any errors. It was indeed a daunting prospect, but I was now supremely confident that I could deliver the goods, as they say. I really had grown up, in flying terms at least. Our B2 category was a provisional rating, which had to be ratified within a year. When ratified the rating was upgraded to B1.

I arrived at Middle Wallop knowing full well that my pass grade at Shawbury was not the best, and filled accordingly with a feeling of not inconsiderable insecurity. My worries were, however, unfounded as, like all new instructors, I was treated with the utmost care. All new embryonic instructors are given a considerable 'bedding in' period, and I was no exception. There were local area famils to be flown and plenty of advice on hand from the more experienced instructors, particularly the flight commanders. I was posted to 'A' Flight, of Advanced Rotary Squadron, the flight responsible for the consolidation of new students, already converted on to the Gazelle, and the start of their military phase of training. Further along the system, they would be passed by us on to 'B' Flight, who were responsible for the final, tactical stage of training. This meant that I was, in effect, still training basic flying skills to reasonably raw students. I loved it. The challenge was tremendous. The students themselves were, just as in my time, a very broad cross section of military rank and background. All were totally dedicated to learning. No teacher could ask for better material. They had already come through the various stages of Basic Fixed Wing training, still carried out on the good old faithful Chipmunk T10, Basic Rotary, to change from Bell 47 G4A to Gazelle, in 1981, so by the time they arrived with us they were well and truly 'blooded.' Initially, the major problem with all the students was the problem of getting used to the incredible difference between the control sensitivity of the Gazelle as opposed to the G4. This was basic flying instruction of the highest order. It took much patience to ease these young men into a Gazelle mentality.

As each new course came through on an eight week cycle, one had the luxury of being able to produce an identical package for each course. We, the instructors, would be allocated one or two students who would, all being well, remain with us for the duration of this phase of the course. There was, however, sufficient flexibility built into the system to allow for a change of instructor, always to the benefit of the student, in the rare situation of a clash of personalities or student response. Some people respond better to one person rather than to another. We are, after all, human. The biggest point was to allow the greatest chance of success to be afforded to the student. We had a system for trying to make the new arrivals at home on their first meeting with us. They would arrive, normally after lunch on their first day on the flight, and be met by the Flight Commander in the main briefing room. We, the instructors, would be waiting outside in the hangar. There were two access doors into the briefing room from the main hangar floor, and across one of these in the briefing room would be placed a backless cupboard. In various forms of fancy dress, we would be called in, through the cupboard, to introduce ourselves. We had great fun with the forms of fancy dress and it always seemed to produce a chuckle or two from the rather apprehensive students. After this performance, the students would be allocated to their instructor. It helped to ease the tension, and made us seem a little more human in their eyes. After a private introductory chat to them, we would then take them out, onto the hangar floor to introduce them to the Gazelle. This for them was a big moment, as it was the aircraft type that they were to spend a lot of time on. Some, at the end of the course, would be streamed onto the Lynx, but only a very few.

We always tried to maintain a close social contact with our students. When they had outside problems, we needed to know about them, as the effect on their flying performance could be dramatic to say the least. We became Mentors in the fullest sense of the word. Of course there were the odd occasions when there was a genuine clash of personalities. We are, after all human beings with all the associated qualities and failings of that race. It is inevitable that from time to time people will grate on each other. When this happened, every possible effort was made to relocate the affected student with another instructor. Of course this also meant that one of the newly selected instructor's students would have to suffer a change and it was never done without this students agreement. The only people that would have to grin and bear any awkward student were the instructors. Different People respond to different stimuli, and one had to be a bit of an amateur psychologist to find the best way of bringing out the best performance. It wasn't always an easy judgement to make. Sometimes it would take maybe a week or more to produce the right 'carrot' without wielding the big stick. This was all part of the great challenge that we Instructors had accepted. There were times when we could have wept for our charges when they struggled to achieve what, for us, was a natural problem easily overcome. There were several, well known, mental barriers that they had to overcome. One of these was hovering. One of the major aerodynamic differences between the Bell G4 and the Gazelle was the fact that the rotors go round in the opposite direction, The Bells go round from left to right, when viewed from below, and the Gazelles from right to left. This means that the opposite tail rotor control pedal has to be applied when power is increased. Let me cast the reader's mind back to my description of my own stumbling efforts, when doing my own flying course back in 1972. Remember what I said about co-ordination? Here were chaps who had been taught that when you increase power, you need to advance the left pedal, now they had to learn to advance the right pedal. Not only that, but the Gazelle sat left skid low in the hover where the Bell G4 had hovered right skid low. All this was very confusing to someone already under tremendous pressure. Another major difference, as already mentioned, was the incredibly sensitive controls of the Gazelle. You only had to think about a minor control movement in the hover, and it had already happened. The control movements in the Bell were relatively coarse. All this took time and lots of patience to impart to these dedicated young men. Their seemingly never-ending resilience always saw them through. If it didn't, we considered it to be our fault, not theirs. It was, indeed, very rare for a student to fall by the wayside during this early part of our phase of training. It would, if it were going to happen at all, happen much later on, either at the end of 'A' flight or during 'B' flight phase.

Having mastered hovering, we would then go on to practice all the various exercises necessary to produce a competent pilot. Cross country flights, pure aircraft handling and night flying would all come in due course, building up to a final handling check with the standards team. It was at this time that I realised how normal I had been when I suffered from testitis. They all did too, pretty well to a man. All one could do was to point this fact out to them and hope that they believed you.

Life for me was, at this time, one of utter fulfilment. I felt that at last I was in a position to give back some of the knowledge that I had amassed over the years. I was also able to try and help these young men not to make some of the stupid mistakes I had made in my early days. I was fast getting the hang of this new found skill, and even had some of the 'review' students passed to me for instruction. The school allowed for a system of review for any student who was experiencing problems with one or more aspects of the course and it did it in the fairest way imaginable. As soon as a problem was diagnosed, the student was warned of the possibility of being put on review. If this had no effect in improvement of the particular area of weakness, then he was placed on review for, normally, a period of five flying hours, in which time every effort would be made by another instructor in place of his own, to correct this fault or faults. If at the end of this period no improvement had been achieved, then the student would be considered for suspension from the course. I have seen grown men break down in tears when this option has been applied. It is, however, probably the most costly military course in the world, and resources are never bottomless. It is in the long run far kinder to suspend a student who has obvious problems, which cannot be rectified, than to allow his hopes to be falsely raised, for the inevitable to happen at a later stage. Thank goodness this didn't happen very often. It was for the new instructor the highest challenge imaginable however, and the 'high' one experienced, seeing the student in question graduate with his wings proudly displayed on his chest at the end of the course, if one were successful, is hard to describe. I had only two review students in five years instructing who failed to make the grade. For these I felt the failure as badly as they did. It can never be a slur on their characters that they did not make the grade. Some people just do not have the ability or physical means to fly. It is a fact of life that is undeniable.

One of the hazards that we were to live with was the persistent manner in which our students tried to kill us each and every day. This could be in a multitude of manners. Nearly each dual sortie ended with practice engine off landings. The helicopter is unique in that, if the engine fails in flight, providing that the correct technique is adopted, one will arrive at the ground in a controlled and safe manner, able to land the aircraft with a minimum of fuss and damage. Let me talk the reader through a typical engine off situation. We are flying at 1,000 feet and 120 knots with everything going normally. Suddenly, it all goes quiet. The engine has stopped. In the twinkling of an eye, we lower the collective lever to reduce the pitch on the rotor blades and enter a state called auto rotation. This in effect means that instead of the engine driving the rotor blades, in simple terms, the airflow coming up through the rotor disc in our descent is driving the blades round much like the blades of a windmill. As long as the rotors retain normal flying RPM then we are flying, albeit downwards. Having selected a suitable landing site, we set the aircraft up using a visual aspect, to land at a particular spot within the capabilities of the descent angle. At about 100 feet above the ground we gently flair the aircraft by easing back on the cyclic stick to reduce our forward speed. This has the extra benefit of increasing the rotor RPM for a number of aerodynamic reasons too complicated to explain in this book without making it a highly technical work. At about 15 to 20 feet we level the aircraft again, now with a much reduced airspeed (somewhere about 20 knots) and using the collective lever, give a gentle check to our rate of descent, gradually increasing the pitch on the rotor blades to smoothly run on at a low forward speed. We have just carried out a successful engine off landing. That is the theory anyway. It is amazing how many variations of a simple theme the average student can devise. If one starts to pull in pitch too high, then the rotor RPM will decay rapidly with the result that there will be insufficient oomph to cushion the run-on landing at the bottom end of the descent. This is a definite no-no. If you don't flair the aircraft in sufficient time, you fail to get rid of the excessive forward speed and finish up by making a pretty good imitation of a Formula 1 racing car. This is also a no-no. If you fail to level the aircraft when approaching the ground you run the risk of striking the tail cone underneath the fin, a resounding thump on good old terra very firma. This normally results in a broken tail cone. It is designed to break on impact, but the servicing team need at least a week's notice in quadruplicate plus a crate of beer if you intend this method of landing. The instructor needs at least a clean pair of underpants providing in advance. On a more serious note, any one of these faults can produce a potentially dangerous situation. It was our job, as instructors, to ensure that the student was not only constantly aware of the possibilities of an engine off situation, but also perfectly capable of handling it should it occur.

I remember one very large Royal Marine student, who tried to kill me in a big way one day. We had entered auto rotation over the engine off area at Middle Wallop after my command "practice engine failure, go," and all was going well until, at about 200 feet the berk started to flair off the speed, and to my utter amazement, started to pull in pitch at the same time. He was very big, a Royal Marines rugby player, and it took all of my strength on the dual collective lever to get it from rising any further. I then had the problem of trying to get up enough forward speed in a rather limited amount of airspace, in order to redeem the now fast decaying rotor RPM. I managed. How I managed, I don't know to this day, but I managed. When we were safely on the ground with everything winding down gently around us, other instructors and students on the engine off area were treated to the comical sight of me beating the said SNCO around the head with the fire extinguisher. He never made that mistake again, and in fact went on to be a very successful pilot. If you ever read this Derek, I hope your headache has gone. I came in for some pretty sick remarks from my fellow instructors who had witnessed the whole thing when I got back to our crew-room. I think it was only my blind instinct for survival that allowed me to convert a potential crash situation into a reasonable engine off landing. Aircraft accidents were very rare at Middle Wallop and I can not remember ever hearing of a student fatality. There were one or two aircraft bent, but not with the loss of life. The last fatal accident that I can remember was with a REME test pilot, when I was on my initial flying course, who crashed into a field near Chilbolton on a hot summer's day in 1972. He crashed, while turning downwind low level, and with two passengers on board. Remember my remarks about the

Sioux being underpowered on a hot day and when near all up weight? Life at Middle Wallop was very hectic. With two students to teach at the same time and a relative shortage of aircraft, competition was keen to book up the aircraft you needed first thing in the morning or, if possible, the evening before. There were between seven and eight instructors on 'A' flight at any one time, and between twelve and fourteen students. This meant that the allocation was not always two to one. Occasionally, you were lucky and had the luxury of a one to one situation which meant that, apart from the odd occasions when you would need to stand in for a brother instructor, whether for health or training reasons, you were in a good position to bring a student along at a cracking pace, and often get ahead of the rest of the course.

With two students, the situation was different however. In the morning you would brief both your charges on the exercise to be flown dual, and then go and fly it with one of them while the other would be given some planning task to occupy his time. One and a half to two hours later you would return with the first student and, while the aircraft was being refuelled, would debrief him over a cup of coffee, and then go straight off with the second to repeat the exercise while the first, if qualified solo at that stage, would go and fly a solo revision sortie covering something already taught. That would take care of the morning. The afternoon would be a repeat of the morning but flying the solo sorties in reverse order. This required two aircraft to be utilised by each instructor at some stage or other of the day. The logistics of providing this degree of availability were, to put it mildly, horrendous, and the Bristows Helicopters engineers, who were responsible for the servicing of the aircraft, were kept at full stretch to meet the demand. They did a marvellous job, and without their co-operation the system would have broken down a long time ago.

After the actual flying side of things, there was the paperwork to complete, this often after the students had gone back to their respective messes for their evening meal. This would be the peaceful time of the day, when we could sit down and gather our thoughts for the reports that had to be written on each student after each dual flying trip. It covered all aspects of the exercise flown with details of strengths and weaknesses displayed by the student. They had to be, at times, brutal. If someone was experiencing a problem over some procedure or other, then it was no use trying to cover it up. It was far better to note it there and then so that it could be concentrated on further later on. Of course, if a particular problem persisted then the option of review might have to be exercised. All this was a terrible responsibility to shoulder. The student's whole future literally hung on our reports. One had to be scrupulously fair. Every two weeks or so would see a night flying session which, in the summer, would not end much before two O'clock in the morning. The one concession to these late and unsociable hours was that we would not have to start before ten O'clock the following morning. It didn't help much, as the rest of the School started flying at eight thirty anyway. Most Friday afternoons, the students being released early for the weekend, we, the instructors, would convene at a local hostelry, the Five Bells at Nether Wallop, for an informal 'Flight Safety Meeting.' Don't be fooled. It was really just an excuse for all of us, or at least, as many as were available, to get together without the students around, to discuss things in general and flying experiences in particular, over a convivial jar of good ale. The Five Bells was strictly out of bounds to any student, who would try to gatecrash on pain of death, or worse. With the chief flying instructor (CFI) present, not too many of them tried it. I feel that in any teaching environment it is imperative that one gets the chance, from time to time, to hide away and not have to worry about being overheard discussing the students' problems with colleagues. I suppose it is a good thing for the instructors to get smashed in private anyway. It probably wouldn't do the students too much good to see just how much good ale the average flying instructor can put away in a relatively short period of time when called upon to do so - and we always responded to the call, believe me!

My time at Middle Wallop as an instructor was undoubtedly the highlight of my flying career. I derived enormous pleasure from having the opportunity to impart some of the knowledge I had gained over the preceding years to those young men who were just embarking on the same path that I had set out on all those years before. I had learnt a lot and, with the same degree of help that I had received, they would succeed also.

Chapter 8.

A Return To Insanity.

May 1982 saw my return to Northern Ireland, this time for a two year tour of duty. I received the news of this posting with very mixed feelings. A four month tour was one thing, but a two year stint was quite another kettle of fish. I understood from my posting order that I was to be posted there as a QHI/Sqn. Pilot. As it turned out that was not exactly the case. I was in fact posted to the PSI flight at RAF Aldergrove. This meant that, as well as doing all the normal and routine tasks that needed to be flown, we also had the responsibility of carrying all the VIPs who visited the province up to and including the Secretary of State. To say that the hours were unsociable is a gross understatement. The pill, however, was sweetened to a great extent by getting to know some extremely interesting people. I think the most tedious facet of this job was the need to be constantly on call. I had to book out every time I left my quarters, no matter for what reason. This restriction, on top of the normal operational parameters within which we were forced to comply, made life very hard to bear at times. Many a time the phone would ring at some ungodly hour and I would be summoned to report in to Aldergrove to fly someone off to one of the more remote outposts of the province. More often than not it would be in the most grotty weather imaginable. It all served to add to the spice of the job I suppose. Life did have its compensations, however, in the form of one or two of my regulars. The most pleasant of these was, without a doubt, the Commander Land Forces, Major General Peter Chiswell. He and his wife were two of the most charming people I think it has ever been my pleasure to meet. He was a Para of the old school and was very protective to all those who supported him. He always referred to us, from his cook to his close protection bodyguard, and even his pilots, as his team. It gave me great pleasure in being thus regarded. On the 29th of December 1982, I was invited to a Christmas party with the Chiswells, with the rest of the team. It was a wonderful affair, with a spirit of close friendship and common purpose. Unfortunately, it was while I was at this party that I received the news that my father was dangerously ill and that I was requested to return to Suffolk as soon as possible. The C.L.F. was very concerned and detailed his Aide to offer me the maximum assistance in obtaining an air ticket and a staff car to meet me at the other end. By 7 O'clock the following morning, I was on the "Red Eye" shuttle out of Aldergrove to Heathrow. Sure enough, there was a staff car to meet me and drive me up to my parents home on the coast of Suffolk. I managed to stay at home with my father until the 28th of December, by which time the Flight back in Northern Ireland were stretched to breaking point, and I had to return. Sadly, my father died on the 7th of January. It was something that I had managed to steel myself to over several years, as his health had been poor for a long time after suffering seven strokes and two heart attacks. Now I had to, once more, return to Suffolk to attend my late fathers funeral. We were very close and it was a terribly sad farewell to someone who was a truly great man. I had in fact discovered, quite by accident, that he had been in the SOE during the 2nd World War, and had been responsible for setting up the escape route for the Polish Government to leave Poland and set up the Polish Government in Exile here, in England. For these services he had been awarded the Polish Gold Cross of Merit 1st Class, which equates to our Victoria Cross. I was indeed very proud of him, and still am.

On the 9th of January I was once more back in Northern Ireland and doing the job I had been trained for. This tour saw me flying more exalted people than I had ever dreamed possible. My log book for this period reads like an extract from Who's Who. Often I would only know at the very last minute who it was I would be flying on any particular sortie. Intermixed with these trips there was still the never ending round of routine jobs to be done around the province. At least on this tour there was a reasonable mix of the ordinary and extraordinary. In June of 1984 I was at last able to leave the six counties for the last time and return to England and Middle Wallop, to complete my last six months of service. Once more I was on the staff at the school as an instructor. I loved this last challenge. I feel that there is no better way to complete a large phase of ones service life than by giving back to the Army some of that which it has bestowed on you. In other words, knowledge. It is, after all, the only way in which flying skills can be passed on to those coming behind you. It always gives me immense pride when I see a young Army pilot at an air show, displaying his skills in the highest traditions of the Corps. I recently had the pleasure of watching a WO2 flying a Lynx helicopter at a major air show in the south, who had been one of my students back in 1984 as a then very young acting sergeant. As long as that rate of progression can continue, I know that the Corps is still in good hands.

I remember very well, my last trip. We had had a very severe thunderstorm over the airfield, and had suffered a direct lightning strike on the Radar Head. This had caused several component units to burn out and as it was in the middle of an intensive instrument training phase for one of the courses, it was imperative that the Radar was serviceable as soon as was humanly possible. I had, at that stage, no more students due to the fact that I was running down, as it were, and I offered to fly the affected units up to the RAF radar servicing unit at North Luffenham in East Anglia. I duly took off with an aircraft full of electronic components about midday, and returned, just as the airfield was about to close for the day, at around 5 O'clock that evening. Before my departure, I had arranged for the mandatory barrel of beer to be laid on in the crew-room so that I could say farewell to all my friends in a civilised way. As I landed, the ground crew rushed up to stow the Gazelle away in the hanger for the night, and I strolled over to the crew-room for a well earned pint or two. Imagine my surprise when, about twenty minutes later, the ground crew made their welcome appearance complete with the cyclic stick head off the aircraft I had just flown. I still have that memento, from Gazelle XZ315, now mounted on a fitting piece of mahogany.

I actually left the Corps in December 1984. It was a rather sad parting as I had derived so much pleasure from my flying days. My entry into civilian life was to prove far harder than I had imagined. But that is another story. As far as the Army Air Corps is concerned, the equipment and aircraft may change as the years roll by, but the spirit of the aviators will always remain in the highest traditions of flying. Military Aviation started in this country with the Army and the Royal Flying Corps and it is right and fitting that it should be continued by a highly professional group of Soldiers who form the new elite - the Army Air Corps to whom my story is dedicated.

EPILOGUE

It is now twenty-five years since I left the Corps. In 1994, the Army Air Corps took over the redundant Royal Air Force station at Wattisham, not very far from my present home at Woodbridge, on the banks of the river Deben. I cannot describe the pleasure and pride I feel every time a Gazelle or Lynx flies over. The distinctive notes of these aircraft still arouses the old feelings of excitement. Now I am on the receiving end of the low flying exercises which take place all around me in this quiet part of East Suffolk. Some people criticise this so called intrusion of their peace. I know the other side of the coin. I understand and appreciate the need for honing skills to a razor sharpness, so that in the event of a need for the exacting and specialised talents of the Army`s pilots, they will not be found wanting.

Living now, as I do, on a Manor Estate, it is fairly common place to witness a flight of anti-tank Lynx, with their director Gazelle working their way into or out of hide positions in this beautiful, rural part of the Suffolk countryside. We now see the awesome sight of the AH64 Apache Longbow, the most powerful anti-tank helicopter in the world, flying round this part of the world, With its very distinctive noise signature I often see them either low flying over the estate or transiting to training sessions at RAF Woodbridge, just down the road as the Army Air Corps moves into the 21st century. Now they are training for deployment to Iraq and Afghanistan. Both 3 and 4 Regiments AAC both operate the Apache to very good effect and both Regiments have seen action over the last two or three years. Every time I witness one go over I think to myself - Go on Hawkeye, keep your eyes keen and your talons sharp. They are

holding up the highest traditions of any Teeth Arm of the British Army.
Since I started to write my story there is much that has happened in the world during the interim period of several years.
The chapters referring to Northern Ireland Operations were written from my memories of the 'Troubles.' Since the Good Friday Agreement, much has changed. I don't think that I could say hand on heart that peace has fully occurred in the province but it is certainly getting there. Despite occasional incidents of terrorism in general terms, life seems to have returned to normal to the extent that my wife and I are considering taking a caravanning holiday in the Province in the near future. Now that is something that we would certainly not have even considered a few years ago. There is much of beauty to see and we would love to enjoy all the sites that are available.

Next of course, Zimbabwe has change out of all resemblance to the Rhodesia that I remember. All of us on the Commonwealth Monitoring force thought that there would be massive changes in the Country once we left after the 'free' elections and President Mugabe took control. Oh dear, we were indeed right. What had been the garden of Africa has now been raped and impoverished to a sad reflection of its former self. Nearly all of the white Rhodesian farmers have been replace by the government with inexperienced and incompetent ex members of the Patriotic Front, with disastrous results. The country simply cannot sustain itself any more. A very sad situation. From a country that produced the very best meat, vegetables, wine, tobacco and fruit in the continent with regular daily flights delivering these goods to South Africa it now produces almost nothing for export. In fact they cannot even feed their own people properly.

Lots has also changed within the Army Air Corps itself. From being branded ‘Teeny weenie Airways’ by our colleagues in the other service, the Corps has now transformed itself into one of the most potent forces to be reckoned with by the Taliban in Afghanistan, in the form of the Apache attack helicopter. Terry Taliban knows and fears them as the Mosquitoes. They strike hard and with a level of accuracy that is awe inspiring. This is the most sophisticated attack helicopter in the world

The last change which I wished with all my heart is the bringing down of the Berlin Wall. When I saw the pictures in the media I have to confess that it brought a tear to my eyes. All that I had done to patrol the Wall in all weathers and with all its risks had come to fruition. At last the East of Germany had now become free from the harsh regime of the Communist East German administration